COLLABORATIONS:
ENGLISH IN OUR LIVES

Intermediate 1 Student Book

The publication of *Collaborations* was directed by the members of the Heinle & Heinle Secondary and Adult ESL Publishing Team:

Editorial Director: Roseanne Mendoza
Production Services Coordinator: Lisa McLaughlin
Market Development Director: Ingrid A. Greenberg

Also participating in the publication of the program were:

Publisher: Stanley Galek
Director of Production: Elizabeth Holthaus
Assistant Editor: Sally Conover
Manufacturing Coordinator: Mary Beth Hennebury
Full Service Design and Production: PC&F, Inc.
Illustration Program: Brain Karas and PC&F, Inc.

Manufactured in the United States of America.

ISBN: 0-8384-4108-4
5   6   7   8   9   04 03 02 01 00

Heinle & Heinle is a division of International Thomson Publishing, Inc.

Photo Credits:

Cover: Jean Bernard-Johnston, top, center left, bottom; Ken Light, center middle; Jann Huizenga, center right.

Unit 1: Jean Bernard-Johnston, 1, 2, 4, 5, 6, 8, 9, 10, 11, 12 right; Jann Huizenga, 12 left.

Unit 2: Metropolitan Canada Convention/Business Center, 17; Jean Bernard-Johnston, 18, 20, 21, 22 bottom, 23, 26, 27, 28 left; Dick Haun, 22 top; Jann Huizenga, 28 right, 29.

Unit 3: San Francisco Convention and Visitors Bureau, photo by Kerrick James, 33 background; Jann Huizenga, 33 top right, 33 bottom right, 39, 43 right, 45; Ken Light, 34, 36, 38, 40; Mark Neyndorff, 43 left.

Unit 4: Silvio Mazzarese, 49; Jann Huizenga, 50, 52, 55, 58 top right, 58 bottom right; Ann Savino, 54; Ken Light, 56; Judy Kaul, 57, 58 left; Jean Bernard-Johnston, 61 left; Nikos Nafpliotis, 61 right.

Unit 5: Jean Bernard-Johnston, 65, 66, 68, 69, 71, 72, 73, 75, 76; Ulli Steltzer, 78 left; Jann Huizenga, 78 right; Bettmann Archive, 70.

Unit 6: James Higgins, 83, 84, 90; Ken Light, 89; Jean Bernard-Johnston, 91, 94, 96; Jann Huizenga, 92, 93, 95 top left, 95 top right; AP/Worldwide Photo, 95 bottom right.

COLLABORATIONS:
ENGLISH IN OUR LIVES

Intermediate 1 Student Book

Jann Huizenga
Jean Bernard-Johnston

Heinle & Heinle Publishers
A Division of International Thomson Publishing, Inc.
Boston, MA 02116, U.S.A.

I T P   The ITP logo is a trademark under license.

CONTENTS

Language Structures	Higher Order Skills and Strategies	Community Building in the Classroom
• present perfect • verbs of intent: *hope, want,* and *would like* + *infinitive* • *should, can* and *could* to make suggestions	• comparing • brainstorming • pooling information • using a map • taking notes in a chart • previewing a text by asking questions • connecting one's life experience with a text	• learning about each other's personal goals • comparing life experiences in North America • helping each other work toward long-term goals
• past continuous • present and past ability with *can/could* and *is/was able to* • information questions with *when, where, why,* and *how often*	• pooling information • comparing • recording information from an Interview • assessing language skills • expressing an opinion • scanning for specific information • trying out new ideas	• learning about each other's experiences with English • sharing ideas for learning outside the classroom • explaining cultural differences
• past with *used to* • *must/have to* • *if* with future possibility	• comparing • analyzing • giving opinions • solving problems • reading a chart • predicting the content of a text from the title • connecting one's own experience with the text	• learning about our families (and the division of chores) • developing a survey with classmates
• present perfect continuous • gerunds and infinitives • direct speech	• pooling information • comparing • guessing meaning from context • giving opinions • predicting the content of a text from the title • brainstorming • evaluating	• learning about our work places • brainstorming small business ideas for customers
• phases of purpose with *to* and *for* • phrases of quantity and proportion (*many, most,* etc.) • comparative adjectives	• listing information • taking notes in a chart • reading place descriptions • comparing specific conditions • making guesses based on visual information • pooling ideas and information • reporting and responding to cultural stereotypes	• learning about our past and present conditions • sharing our knowledge of community resources • identifying community problems and suggesting possible solutions
• exclamatory sentences • connecting ideas with *when, before* and *after* • connecting ideas with *because*	• summarizing • taking notes • writing in chronological order • predicting the content of a text from the title • expressing opinions • categorizing • giving reasons • guessing meaning from context	• learning about our trips to North America • learning about our reasons for immigrating • expressing our feelings about life in North America • teaching about our countries

THE WORLD

Do you want to see where the people in this book come from? Their countries are labeled.

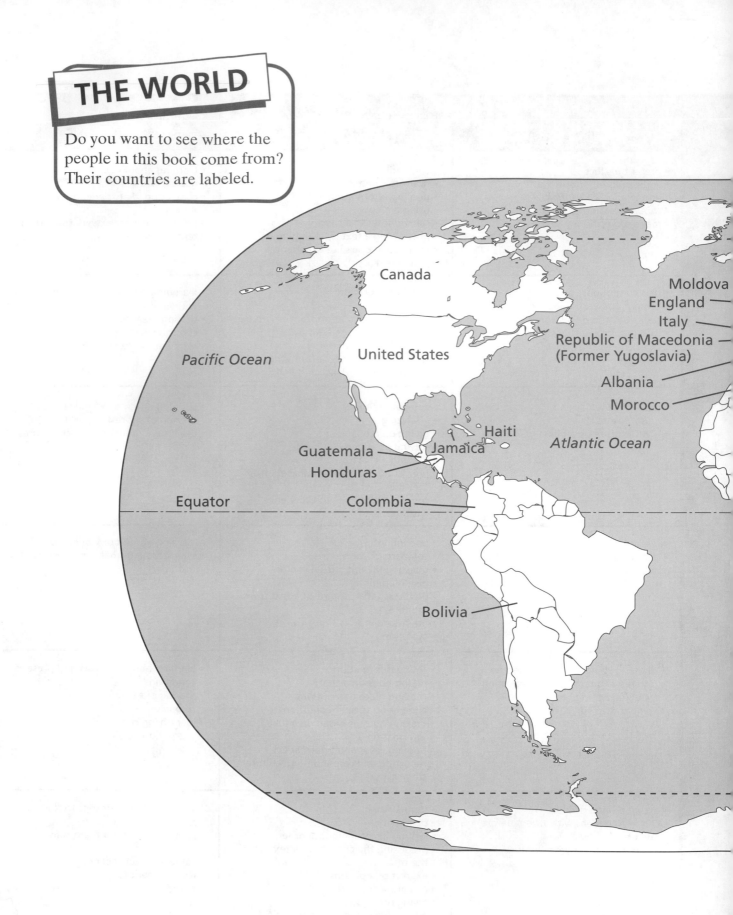

Canada

Moldova
England
Italy
Republic of Macedonia
(Former Yugoslavia)
Albania
Morocco

Pacific Ocean

United States

Haiti

Guatemala
Jamaica
Honduras

Atlantic Ocean

Equator

Colombia

Bolivia

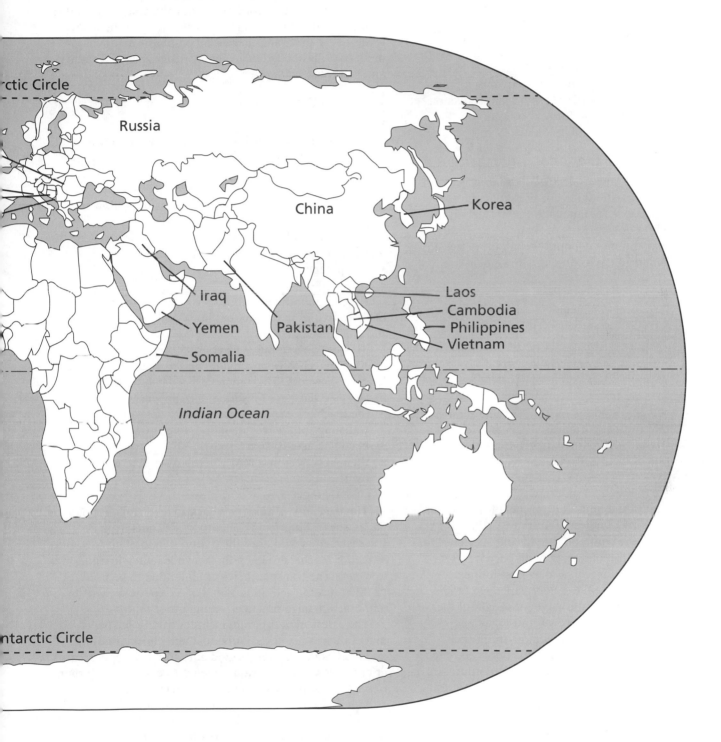

Arctic Circle

Russia

China

Korea

Iraq

Yemen

Pakistan

Laos

Cambodia

Philippines

Vietnam

Somalia

Indian Ocean

Antarctic Circle

ABOUT THIS SERIES

Our purpose for creating this series is to provide opportunities for adult immigrants and refugees to develop English language and literacy skills while reflecting, as individuals and with others, on their changing lives.

We believe that the best adult ESL classrooms are places where learners and teachers work collaboratively, talk about issues that matter to them, use compelling materials, and engage in tasks that reflect their life experiences and concerns. We see learning as a process in which students are encouraged to participate actively, and the classroom as a place where students share and reflect on their experiences and rehearse for new roles in the English-speaking world beyond its walls.

How are the books in the series organized?

Unlike most adult ESL materials, *Collaborations* is not organized around linguistic skills nor life skill competencies, but around contexts for language use in learners' lives. Each student book consists of six units, beginning with the individual and moving out through the series of ever-widening language environments shown below.

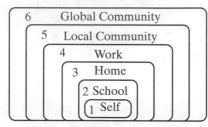

The units revolve around the narratives of newcomers who tell or write of their experiences. Each unit focuses on a particular site in North America, generally one that has a significant number of ESL programs and learners. In some locations, we have chosen a particular ethnic group. In others, we have made the multiethnic character of the area the focal point of the unit. It is our belief that within the marvelous diversity of newcomers, there are seeds for finding similarities—the common threads of experience—as newcomers make sense of managing life in a new setting with new constraints as well as new possibilities.

Grammar, vocabulary development, language functions, and competencies are interwoven throughout the units in each student book. However, the organizing principles are reversed from those of most traditional materials. Rather than selecting linguistic items and then creating contexts to elicit them, *Collaborations* addresses language development and competencies as they naturally emerge from the contexts and the authentic texts. For those who wish to focus more on specific competencies or language structures, detailed indexes are provided to enable participants to identify where the item is taught, and where resources for further practice can be found.

Collaborations is intended for use with learners of English in adult programs in school districts, community colleges, and community-based programs. While it is an excellent fit in non-credit programs, it may also be the right choice for some credit programs because of its strong emphasis on critical thinking and problem solving. The assessment component for the program—with its placement guidelines and instructions for portfolio assessment as well as more formal quizzes and tests—facilitates adaptation to either program. Particularly at the higher levels of the program, there is an emphasis on development of skills needed in academic programs, GED study, and workplace situations.

What are the other components of *collaborations*?

The supplementary **workbook** for each level is correlated to the student book. It offers independent study tasks that recycle and reinforce language points from the corresponding units of the student book. Each workbook unit has a predictable structure that contains the following:
- grammar work in context
- extended reading and writing
- vocabulary work
- competency-based tasks
- tests and self assessment

In each unit, the workbook tasks follow the sequence of the activities in the student book and further develop the unit themes.

The **teacher's resource kit** consists of a variety of materials to extend classroom activities and to facilitate and assess learners' progress. The materials listed below are provided in a format that can be inserted into the teacher's kit binder.
- the teacher's edition
- wall maps of the world and of North America
- blackline activity masters
- the assessment program
- overhead transparencies
- cassette tapes

The teacher's edition includes reduced student book pages, suggestions from the authors, insights from field test instructors who used the material in their classes, and space for teachers to keep their own teaching/learning journals. The transparencies are intended to be used for problem-posing activities, Language Experience writing, and oral language practice, among other things.

The assessment program includes traditional benchmarks such as pre-tests, individual unit checks, midterm and final exams, as well as guidelines for developing learner portfolios. The program is meant to encourage learners to set their own goals and monitor their own progress.

Finally, there are two cassette tapes for each level. The classroom tape contains all the stories from each unit of the student book as well as an authentic "review interview," for which there is an accompanying worksheet in the teacher's kit. The student tape contains all of the above with additional listening activities for use at home or in a lab.

Each unit in the student book is designed to provide at least 10 hours of activities, or 60 hours for the entire book. However, if used in conjunction with the workbook and teacher's kit, each unit provides at least 16 hours of activities for a total of 96 hours.

ABOUT THIS LEVEL

What is included in each unit?

Each unit in this level includes:

- authentic texts of some kind (photos, writings, interview material) that have been collected from newcomers throughout the United States and Canada;
- an opportunity to react/respond to those texts and to relate them to personal experience;
- an invitation to master the language of the first text in each unit by *Playing with Story Language;*
- an interactive *Learning About Each Other* task to foster fluency while building community among learners in the classroom;
- *Doing It in English* tasks, in which learners practice functions of English for purposes appropriate to each context;
- a focus on *Ideas for Action* in which learners reflect critically on their situations and what they can do to act on them;
- an opportunity for *Journal Writing,* which allows students to react in writing to the themes of the unit and interact on paper with the teacher;
- *Other Voices from North America* and non-prose readings (schedules, graphs and charts) to provide expanded opportunities for discussion and for developing reading strategies;
- *Reading Strategy* and *Learning Strategy* boxes which highlight useful study strategies and bring them to conscious awareness;
- an *Options for Learning* task, in which students choose to study one or more life skills from a list of competencies (and follow up with worksheets in the Teacher's Kit);
- an opportunity to develop one's own *Word Bank* at the end of each unit;
- an invitation to *Look Back,* where learners reflect on what they have learned, what they want to study more about, and which activities suit them the most; and
- a *Checklist for Learning* to provide learners with a way to monitor their own progress and to review previous material.

QUESTIONS ABOUT *COLLABORATIONS*

The language in this book is not as controlled as other materials I've used. Will this be too difficult for my students?

Adults have been learning languages, with and without language instruction, from the time of the first human migration. Students in an English-language setting acquire language most efficiently when there is something worth communicating about. When the building blocks of language are made accessible, acquisition becomes natural and pleasurable. The aim in this series is to provide learners with the tools they need and to create conditions in which communicating is well worth the effort. Because language is a medium for negotiating social relationships, part of the goal is to create a classroom community in which English takes on meaning and purpose. The obstacles learners face because of their incomplete mastery of the English in the material are more than offset by compelling reasons to communicate.

What should I do if my students do not yet know the grammar or vocabulary in the stories and tasks?

Any teacher who has ever faced a class of eager ESL learners has had to grapple with the reality that learners come with differences in their prior exposure to English and with their own individual language-learning timetables, strategies, and abilities. There is no syllabus which will address directly and perfectly the stage of language development of any particular learner, let alone a diverse group. This material reflects the belief that learners can benefit most when forms and functions are made available in the service of authentic communicative tasks. Teaching is most effective when it taps into areas that are ready for development.

For this reason, tasks in *Collaborations* are open-ended and multi-faceted, allowing individuals to make progress according to their current stages of development. The inclusion of numerous collaborative tasks makes it possible for more capable peers as well as instructors to provide assistance to learners as they move to new stages of growth in mastering English.

It is not necessary for learners to understand every word or grammatical structure in order to respond to a story, theme, or issue. The context created by evocative photographs, by familiar situations, and by predictable tasks usually allows learners to make good guesses about meaning even when they do not control all of the vocabulary or structures they see. Any given reading or activity is successful if it evokes a reaction in the learner, and if it creates a situation in which learners are eager to respond. When appropriate language structures and vocabulary are provided toward that end, language acquisition is facilitated. Within this framework, total mastery is not critical: total engagement is.

What do I do about errors my students make?

Errors are a natural part of the language-learning process, as learners test out their hypotheses about how the new language works. Different learners benefit from varying degrees of attention to form and function. For this reason, there are supplementary activities in the workbooks and teacher's kits where learners can give focused attention to vocabulary, grammar, functions, and competencies. The detailed indexes can also assist users in locating language forms that are of immediate concern to them. Form-focused activities can be used as material for explicit study or practice, as well as for monitoring progress in language development. This series operates on the assumption that the most important ingredient for language acquisition is the opportunity to use English to communicate about things that matter. The supplementary materials will be most effective if the time set aside to focus on form is not seen as an end in and of itself, but rather, is viewed as a necessary component in developing the tools for meaningful communication and classroom community-building.

ACKNOWLEDGMENTS

This book would never have been possible without the enthusiastic help of those whose stories grace these pages. We cannot thank them all by name here, but their names appear after each story. We are grateful to colleagues, teachers, and administrators who helped so much in arranging interviews and collecting stories, among them Ana Macias (El Paso Community College, TX); Nancy Gross (LaGuardia Community College, NYC); Jon Yasin (Bergen Community College, NJ); Andrzej Pietrzak (Toronto Metropolitan Separate School Board, Canada); Andrew Livingston (Nelson, Canada); Jolanta Klimaszewski (Holy Name School, Toronto); Laura Negrotto (LaSalle Adult Education Program, Toronto); Bona Tep (Greenfield Community College, MA); Harriet Lindenburg (Santa Fe Community College, NM); Norma Tecson (Filipino Training Center, San Francisco); Youn Chey (Korean Center, San Francisco); David Park (Korean Community Center, San Francisco); and Marta Pitts (Lindsey Hopkins Technical Education Center, Miami).

We'd like to thank the other members of the original "think tank," Gail Weinstein-Shr, Marilyn Gillespie, Jean Handscombe, and Loren McGrail, whose valuable input kicked the project off, as well as our reviewers along the way, all of whom gave shape to the final product. Our many field testers allowed us to quote them extensively in the Teacher's Edition, and we are thankful for their wonderful insights.

At Heinle, the authors are grateful to Editorial Director Roseanne Mendoza for her expert guidance; to Lisa McLaughlin, Production Editor, for her sensational work in producing the series; and to Stan Galek and Charles Heinle for believing in this project from the start. We'd also like to thank Louise Gelinas and the staff at PC&F for their fine editing and production work.

Last, but not least, the support of our families and friends is warmly appreciated. Jean is grateful to Jon and Sarah for the wise counsel and warm hospitality, and to Eliot Luke for his stalwart assistance in shouldering tape recorders and camera equipment for his mom. Special thanks also to Sadette for the loan of an umbrella on a very wet day in Toronto. Jann would like to thank Kim for the laughter, love, and help with photography, John and Dolly for their encouragement and support, and Mia Thomas-Ruzic for sharing inspiration and ideas on teaching reading.

Unit 1

Looking Ahead in Paramus, New Jersey

The stories in this unit are from northern New Jersey. New Jersey is a small state, but it has one of the largest immigrant populations in North America.

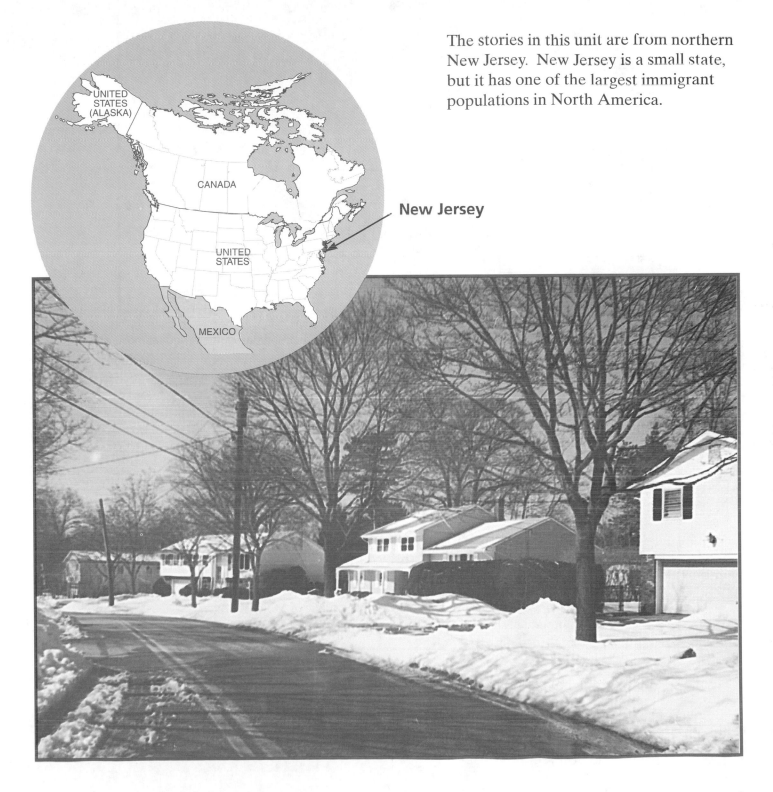

Marianna Yasskaya's Story

In my country, there were no opportunities to go back to school at my age. After working all day, I had to stay at home and be a housewife.

I have been here almost three years now. When I first came, I missed my country a lot. I didn't know any English at all. But now, I feel young again. I have been in this class since September. I am a lot more confident. It still takes me a long time to find the right words, but I have learned to express myself a little bit. Learning a new language is like having a window on the world!

I am not sure about my future. I think it is going to be hard for me to find a good job, but I will try.

Marianna Yasskaya studies English at Bergen Community College (BCC) in Paramus, New Jersey. She is originally from the Republic of Moldova. In this photograph, she is in the computer writing lab at the college.

IDIOM
window on the world

- How long have you been in North America?

- How did you feel when you first arrived in North America?

- How do you feel now?

2 Playing with Story Language

Follow these steps:

A. Listen to the whole story.

B. Listen again and repeat each sentence.

C. Write in the missing words.

D. Listen one more time. Check the words you wrote.

In my country, there were no opportunities to _____*go*_____ back to school at
                                                        1

my age. After working all day, I _____ to stay at home and be a housewife.
                                          2

I have been here almost three years now. When I first _____, I missed
                                                              3

my country a lot. I didn't _____ any English at all. But now, I
                                  4

_____ young again. I have been in this _____ since
        5   6

September. I am a lot more confident. It still takes me a long time to find the right

words, but I have learned _____ express myself a little bit. Learning a new
                                  7

language is like having a window on the world!

I _____ not sure about my future. I think it is going to be hard for me to
        8

_____ a good job, but I will try.
        9

E. Read the question. Write two more questions about the story.

1. _____How long has Marianna been here?_____

2. _____

3. _____

F. Ask a partner to answer all three questions without looking at the story.

Learning about
Each Other: Connecting Past and Present

I **have lived** in New Jersey for almost three years. I **have been** in this class since September.

A. Work with a partner. Ask these questions.
  How long have you lived here?
  How long have you studied English?
  How long have you been in this class?

Periods of Time	
for three years for a long time	**for** + length of time
since 1992 since last Friday	**since** + point in time

How long have you lived here?

I have lived here for a long time.

B. Write one sentence about yourself and one about your partner.

I have _____

My partner has _____

Present Perfect Verbs					
I You We They	have	lived studied known been	She He	has	lived studied known been
Use **present perfect** verbs to tell what happened during a period of time that started in the past and continues to the present.					

4 Doing It in English: Expressing Long-Term Goals

A. Read what two of Marianna's classmates hope to do in the future.

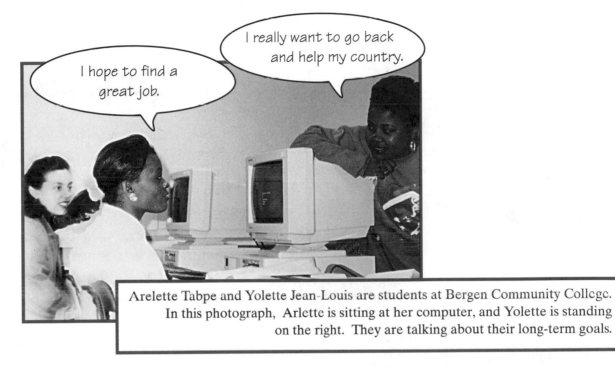

Arelette Tabpe and Yolette Jean-Louis are students at Bergen Community College. In this photograph, Arlette is sitting at her computer, and Yolette is standing on the right. They are talking about their long-term goals.

B. Below are some other goals of Marianna's classmates. Which ones are your goals too? Check (✔) them.

_____ find a great job
_____ go back and help my country
_____ buy a house of my own
_____ give my children a good education
_____ live in a safe place
_____ start my own business

C. Brainstorm with your class. Make a list of your classmates' long-term goals.

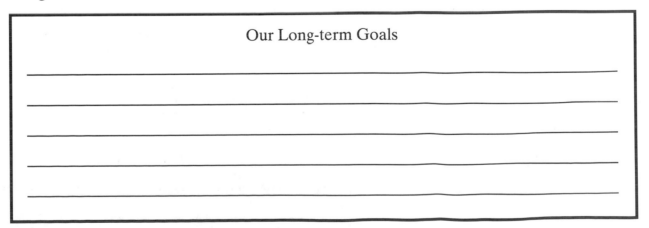

Our Long-term Goals

D. Rodney Oh is Marianna Yasskaya's classmate. Read about his long-term goal. Is his dream similar to yours?

Similar ❑   Different ❑

My Dream
Everybody has different goals and dreams. My dream is to become a businessman. Someday I want to manage a successful company. That is why I am here at a community college. I know that there are many things I have to learn to survive in this country, so I have to learn everything I can to help me reach this goal.

Rodney Oh is from Korea. In this photograph, he is writing a paper about his long-term goals in the computer lab at BCC with the help of his teacher, Jon Yasin.

⑤ Journal Writing

In your journal, write about one of your long-term goals. What would you like to be able to do sometime in your life? Do you think it is going to be easy or difficult? Why?

Verbs to Express Long-Term Goals	
want expect hope plan would like would love	+ INFINITIVE (*to get, to go, to have*)

6 Sharing Information: Where We Come from

A. Some of Marianna Yasskaya's classmates did not know anything about her country, so she wrote the paragraph below. Read it once and look at the map.

B. Read the paragraph again. This time, circle the words and expressions that are new for you. Discuss your questions with the class.

> **Learning Strategy**
>
> Use the map to help you find the places in the paragraph.

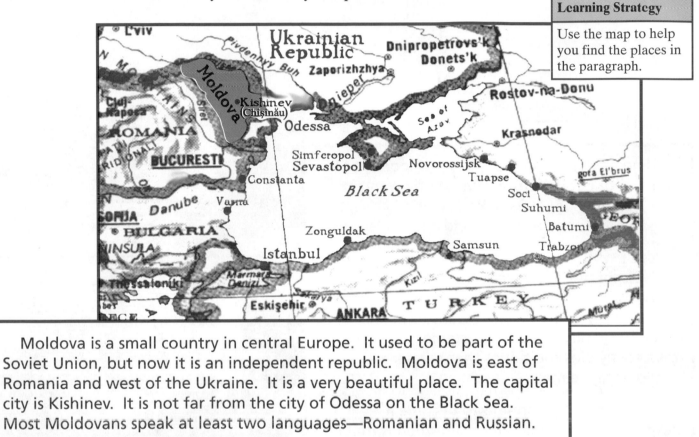

Moldova is a small country in central Europe. It used to be part of the Soviet Union, but now it is an independent republic. Moldova is east of Romania and west of the Ukraine. It is a very beautiful place. The capital city is Kishinev. It is not far from the city of Odessa on the Black Sea. Most Moldovans speak at least two languages—Romanian and Russian.

C. Write the things you know about your country on the left side. Then ask a partner about his or her country. Write information about your partner's country on the right.

My Country	My Partner's Country
Name:	Name:
Capital:	Capital:
Location:	Location:
Size:	Size:
Other information:	Other information:

7 More Stories from New Jersey

A. Look at the picture and read the information about Julio Bello under the story. Think of some questions about Julio Bello before you begin to read his story. Write one of your questions here.

_____

_____

Reading Strategy

Asking questions before you begin to read can help you understand the story better.

Time goes by really fast, so it's important to think about your future. Everybody wants to live a comfortable life. Like everybody else, I'd like to have enough to eat and a nice place to live.

I've thought a lot about my future, what I want to do with my life. I'd like to work at a job that's interesting, and I want to make enough money to be comfortable. I want to give to my kids the things that my parents could not give me.

Right now I'm planning to become a respiratory therapist. The main thing is that I want to keep on feeling proud of myself.

Julio Bello is from Cuba. He is a student at Bergen Community College. He also works full time as a security guard.

IDIOM
make money

B. Look at the picture and read the information about Yolette at the bottom of the story. What do you hope to find out in her story? Write one question.

_____

I have lived in this country for most of my life, but I still remember a lot about Haiti. Our culture was very warm. You didn't have to lock your doors all the time, like you do here. You could just walk in and out of the neighbors' houses. They all took care of you.

There are a lot of Haitians in New Jersey now —I would say about 30,000. Most of the older people are struggling just to provide for their families. They take any job they can find, like working in factories and washing dishes in restaurants. My mother had to work really hard cleaning other people's houses so I could go to school.

Haitians in my generation are trying hard to get a good education. We want to go back and do something to help our country. Together, I believe we can make a real difference.

Yolette Jean-Louis is from Haiti. Her native language is Creole. She has lived in New Jersey for most of her life.

> **IDIOM**
> make a difference

C. **What about you?**

	YES	NO
I think about the future a lot.	☐	☐
I'd like to work at a job that's interesting.	☐	☐
I remember a lot about my country.	☐	☐
People have to lock their doors in my country.	☐	☐
I usually lock my doors here.	☐	☐
I would like to go back and do something to help my country.	☐	☐

8 Doing It in English: Making Suggestions to Newcomers

A. What suggestions can you give people from your country who have just arrived in North America? Read Julio Bello's answer.

They shouldn't feel embarrassed about their English. Just look around. There are a lot of people just like them.

B. Work with a small group. Tell the group where you are from. Explain what advice you would give to newcomers from your country. Add to the list of suggestions from Julio Bello's class.

Name & Country	Advice
Arlette, Ivory Coast	They can find friendly people to talk to.
Hassan, Palestine	They should ask a lot of questions.

Making Suggestions		
They	should can could	ask a lot of questions.

C. Do you remember Rodney Oh's long-term goal? His classmates made these two suggestions to help him become a successful businessman. Discuss them with your group. Then add one suggestion of your own.

He should work very hard.

He should make a lot of friends.

_____

Rodney Oh and friends at Bergen Community College.

D. Ask your group to suggest ways to work toward one of your long-term goals. Explain what your goal is and what you are already doing. Write their suggestions below.

My goal: _____

What I am doing now: _____

My classmates' suggestions:

_____

_____

_____

9 Other Voices from North America

A. Work with a partner. Choose one of the stories to read. After two minutes, close your book and retell the story to your partner.

B. Read the other story.

C. Circle the words you want to remember.

I'm from Tegucigalpa, Honduras. I'm single now, but I want to get married, although I'm still in my twenties.

One of my goals is to become a great businessman. That's why I'm studying English now. I have to do this because I would like to solve some of my country's problems, like poverty and its economy.

About me, I can say that I haven't been around too long, but I know the difference between the good things and the bad.

Roberto Meija studies ESL at Lindsey Hopkins Technical Education Center in Miami, FL.

> **IDIOM**
> been around

I've been here 14 years. That's long enough to feel the cold. My body is losing energy. I miss my country every day. I dream about it every night.

One day, I would like to return to see my country again. I want to visit my relatives and stay in the house where I was born. I don't know when it will be possible, who can say? We never know what's going to happen in the future, but we can dream.

Thuy Trang lives in Toronto, Ontario, Canada, and is originally from Vietnam. She is a full-time legal assistant and a part-time professional singer. In this picture, she is singing at the Sacred Mountain Buddhist Temple in Toronto.

10 Ideas for Action: Reaching a Common Goal

A. Work in a small group. Talk about your long-term goals. Find one goal you all have in common. Write it here.

_____

B. Brainstorm with the group. Think of some things that will help you reach this common goal. Make a list of your group's ideas below.

1. _____

2. _____

3. _____

4. _____

5. _____

C. With your group, choose one idea you all like best. Tell the class.

11 Bringing the Outside in: News from Our Countries

A. Make a list of your classmates' native countries. Locate these countries on a world map, and list the capital city of each country on the board.

B. Search through a newspaper or news magazine. Look for headlines that have the names of your classmates' countries. Cut out the headlines and pin them on a bulletin board. Talk about why these countries are in the news.

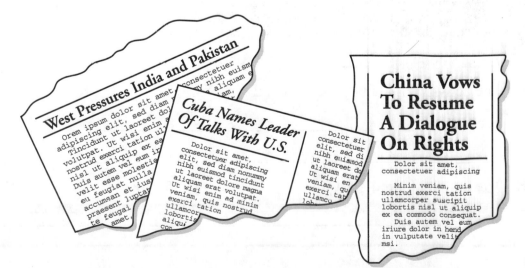

12 Word Bank

Choose four new words or expressions from this unit that you want to remember. Use them in sentences of your own.

Example:

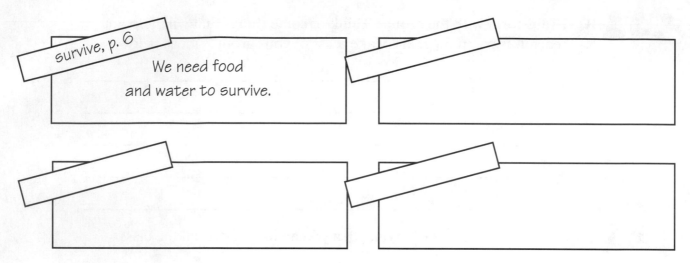

survive, p. 6

We need food
and water to survive.

13 Looking Back

Think about your learning. Complete this form. Then tell the class your ideas.

A. The most useful thing I learned in this unit was _____

_____ .

B. I would still like to learn _____ .

C. I learned the most by working

_____ alone.   _____ with a partner.   _____ with a group.

D. The activity I liked best was   1   2   3   4   5   6   7   8   9   10   11   12

because _____ .

_____ .

E. The activity I liked least was   1   2   3   4   5   6   7   8   9   10   11   12

because _____ .

Checklist for Learning

I. Vocabulary: Check (✔) the words and phrases you know. Add more words and phases if you wish. For extra practice, write sentences with the words.

Words to Express Goals

_____ get
_____ find
_____ help
_____ buy
_____ give
_____ start
_____ become
_____ _____

IDIOMS

_____ window on the world
_____ make money
_____ make a difference
_____ been around

Occupations

_____ business person
_____ manager
_____ housewife
_____ respiratory therapist
_____ singer
_____ legal assistant
_____ _____
_____ _____

Words to Express Feelings

_____ confident
_____ proud
_____ safe
_____ embarassed
_____ _____
_____ _____

Countries

_____ Korea
_____ Canada
_____ Haiti
_____ Vietnam
_____ Honduras
_____ Cuba
_____ Ukraine
_____ _____
_____ _____

II. Language: Check (✔) what you can do in English. Add more ideas if you wish.

I can

_____ express my long-term personal goals.
_____ tell how long I have lived somewhere or done something.
_____ read short descriptive passages about different countries.
_____ describe where I come from.
_____ ask information questions before I begin to read.
_____ make suggestions to people about how to reach their goals.
_____ _____
_____ _____

III. Listening: Listen to the Review Interview at the end of Unit 1. Ask your teacher for the *Collaborations* worksheet.

Unit 2

Trying It Out in Toronto, Ontario

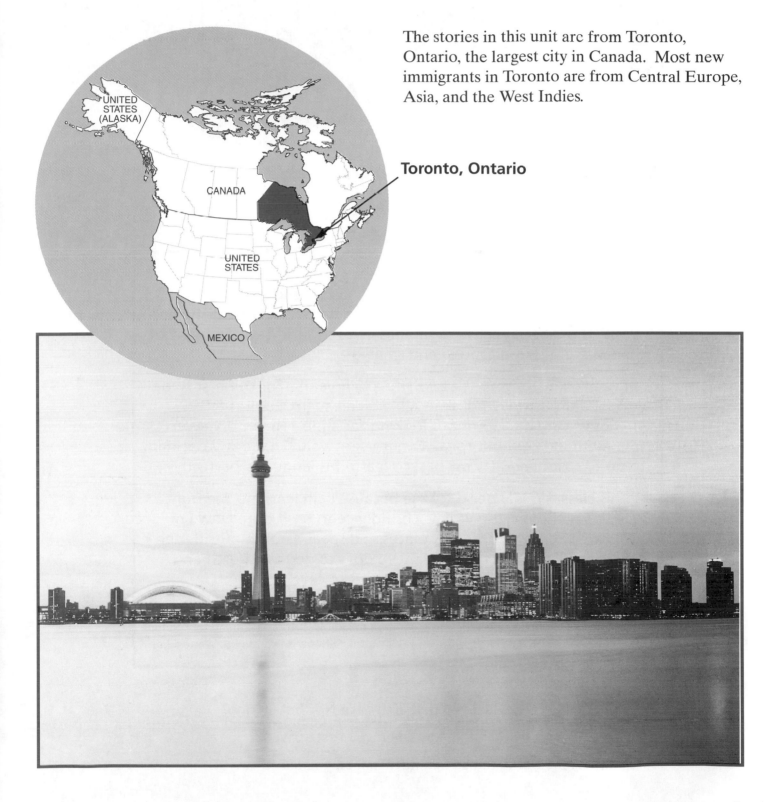

The stories in this unit arc from Toronto, Ontario, the largest city in Canada. Most new immigrants in Toronto are from Central Europe, Asia, and the West Indies.

Toronto, Ontario

Sadette Cakalli's Story

When I first came to Canada, I was scared of everything. Actually, I didn't speak one word of English. When we were growing up in Albania, they only told us bad things about the West. The first day I saw Canadians I was so surprised. So many of them were walking around and smiling!

I've lived in Toronto for two and a half years. For the first two years, I didn't study English at all. I didn't speak English to anybody. One day, I was out looking for a job. The interviewer told me that I couldn't speak English very well. That day, I decided to go to school and try my best to learn this language perfectly.

This class is really good for me because I am learning the right way to say things. It gives me confidence to try it out. Now I'm not scared to go to different places and speak English outside the classroom. The next thing I want to do is to go to a church and join a choir. I think I have a really good voice!

Sadette Cakalli is from Albania, where she was trained as a professional opera singer. Now she is a student in the adult ESL program at Holy Name School in Toronto. In this photo, Sadette is listening to the teacher.

• What surprised you when you first arrived in North America?

• How much English did you know when you first arrived?

• What are some of the things that have helped you learn?

2 Playing with Story Language

Follow these steps:

A. Close your eyes and listen to the whole story. Listen again to the second paragraph.

B. Write the words in correct order in the blanks. Don't look back at page 18!

I've lived in Toronto ___*for two and a half years*_____.
two   years   half   and   a   for

For the first two years, _____.
English   I   all   speak   didn't   at

I didn't speak English to anybody. One day, I was out _____
a   looking   job   for

_____. The interviewer told me that I

_____. That day,
couldn't   well   English   very   speak

I decided to go to school and try my best to _____
perfectly   learn   language   this

_____.

C. Work with a partner. Read the paragraph aloud. Discuss any differences. Look back at the story to check your sentences.

D. With your partner, think of a good question about this paragraph. Write both the question and answer in the box. Try your question out on some other classmates.

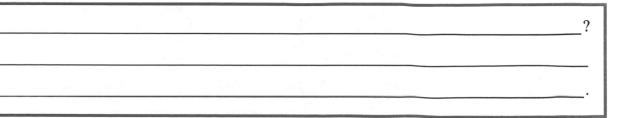

Doing It in English: Telling about Decisions

> I **was** out **looking** for a job when I decided to study English.

Past Continuous		
I He She	**was**	**looking** for a job.
We You They	**were**	

Past continuous verbs tell what was going on when something else happened.

A. Think about an important decision *you* have made. What did you decide? Where were you living at the time? What were you doing? Tell a partner.

> I decided to move to Toronto.

> Where were you living then?

> I was living in Detroit.

> What were you doing when you decided?

> I was watching TV.

B. Tell the class about your partner's decision.

4 Learning about Each Other: Our Experiences with English

A. How well could you speak English when you first arrived in North America? Read these answers from two of Sadette Cakalli's classmates.

> I could read and write fairly well, but I wasn't able to understand people when they talked to me. I could only answer 'yes' or 'no.'

> I could understand a lot, but I couldn't speak correctly. I was able to read some textbooks in English, but I didn't have a chance to read newspapers or magazines.

Expressing Ability and Inability	
Present	Past
(I) can cannot	could could not
(I) am able to am not able to	was able to was not able to

B. Interview a partner. Ask about your partner's past and present abilities in English. Mark your partner's responses on the chart below.

> How well could you speak English when you first arrived?

> Not very well.

Partner's Name _____

0 = not at all
1 = not very well
2 = fairly well
3 = very well
4 = perfectly

On Arrival

	0	1	2	3	4
speak	☐	☐	☐	☐	☐
understand	☐	☐	☐	☐	☐
read	☐	☐	☐	☐	☐
write	☐	☐	☐	☐	☐

Now

	0	1	2	3	4
speak	☐	☐	☐	☐	☐
understand	☐	☐	☐	☐	☐
read	☐	☐	☐	☐	☐
write	☐	☐	☐	☐	☐

Sharing Ideas: Ways to Learn Outside the Classroom

A. These are some of the ways Sadette's classmates like to practice their English outside the classroom. Check the things that are also helpful to you. Then brainstorm with your class. Add more activities to the list.

_____ join a sports team
_____ go to a Karaoke bar
_____ watch television
_____ go to the movies
_____ listen to the radio
_____ listen to tapes
_____ make friends with North Americans
_____ marry a North American
_____ read simple books
_____ read the newspaper

_____ _____

_____ _____

_____ _____

 B. Look over the list again. What do you already do? What would you like to try? How do you think these activities will improve your English? Tell a partner.

6 Doing It in English: Explaining a Method

A. Sadette Cakalli has a special method for improving her English at home. Do you think it would be a good method for you? Why or why not?

Actually, I watch TV a lot. I like to watch soap operas. My favorite show is *The Bold and the Beautiful.* I love it. It's on every day from 3:00 to 3:30. If my friends call me during this time, I say, 'Sorry, I can't talk now.'

The language the actors use is very clear, and they speak very slowly. They show everything that they do, so it's really easy to understand.

I buy this magazine every week. It helps me understand what's happening on TV. I read the magazine right after I see the show.

B. Discuss Sadette's method with a partner. Ask and answer questions that begin with the question words in circles.

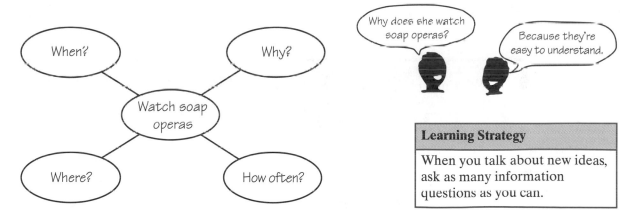

Why does she watch soap operas?

Because they're easy to understand.

When?   Why?

Watch soap operas

Where?   How often?

Learning Strategy

When you talk about new ideas, ask as many information questions as you can.

C. Think about your favorite method for learning English outside the classroom. Explain it to a partner. Answer all of your partner's questions.

D. What do you think of your partner's method? Write your opinion here.

I think

Journal Writing

Write about *your* experiences learning English. How well did you communicate in English when you first arrived in North America? What are your special methods for learning English outside the classroom? How does your English class help you?

Sharing Experiences: Cultural Differences

A. When Sadette doesn't want to talk to someone on the telephone, she says, "Sorry, I can't talk to you now." When is it important to say "I'm sorry" in your culture? When do North Americans apologize? Fill in the chart below.

Ways of Apologizing
I'm sorry. . .
Excuse me. . .
Forgive me. . .

Ways of Responding
It's OK.
That's all right.
It doesn't matter.
Don't worry about it.
Never mind. These things happen.

Do people usually apologize when they	In North America		In Your Country	
	YES	NO	YES	NO
can't talk to someone?	☐	☐	☐	☐
are late for something?	☐	☐	☐	☐
interrupt someone?	☐	☐	☐	☐
forget something?	☐	☐	☐	☐
bump into someone?	☐	☐	☐	☐
make a lot of noise?	☐	☐	☐	☐
call the wrong number?	☐	☐	☐	☐

B. Have you ever been surprised or confused when someone apologized to you? Have you ever been upset or angry because someone didn't apologize? Tell the class about your experience.

Think It Over: Choosing TV Programs

A. The average North American watches television 35 hours per week. How many hours a week do you watch? What programs do you like? Why do you like them? Discuss your ideas with the class.

B. Look at this schedule of TV programs from *The Toronto Globe and Mail*. Underline the programs you would like to watch.

MONDAY JUNE 6

AFTERNOON

Noon

(2) Flintstones (CC)
(4) News
(6)(41) News at Noon (CC)
(7)(9)(11)(13) News (CC)
(13) Cocotte Minute
(17) Sesame Street (CC)
(19) Living With Your Teenager
(25) Le Midi
(29) Designing Women (CC)
(47) Perfect Strangers (CC)
(57) LunchTelevision
(AE) Police Story
(FA) Walt Disney Presents
(MM) Intimate & Interactive With Heart 937877
(SBK) The Honeymooners
(TBS) (12:05) Perry Mason
(TLC) Yvonne's Cookbook
(TMN) Movie: ★★★ Tous les Matins du Monde (biography, 1991) (To 2 p.m.) 525877
(TNN) Aleene's Creative Living
(TSN) SportsDesk (CC)
(V) Forever Green
(WGN) Geraldo
(YTV) Brownstone Kids (CC)

12:30

(2) People's Court
(4) The Young and the Restless (CC) 972709
(7) Loving (CC) 78506
(13) Azimuts
(25) Le Jour J 50 Ans Apres
(29) M*A*S*H
(47) Out of This World
(SBK) Beverly Hillbillies
(TLC) Biba's Italian Kitchen
(TSN) Auto Racing IndyCar

Miller Genuine Draft 200. (To 2:30 p.m.) 811612
(YTV) OWL/TV (CC)

1:00

(2)(6)(41) Days of Our Lives (CC) 51815 79235 319457
(7) All My Children (CC) 66761
(9)(13) CTV News: The Road to Normandy (To 2 p.m.) 64490 17506
(11) Night Heat
(13) Voies du Developpement
(17) The Great Eclipse 39322
(19) D-Day: The Shortest Day See 8 p.m.
(29) Dear John (CC)
(47) Neighbours 577544
(57) Movie: ★★★ Battleground (war, 1949) Van Johnson. (To 3:30 p.m.) 746709
(AE) Rockford Files (CC)
(CNN) Larry King Live See 9 p.m. (To 2:30 p.m.) (CC)
(FA) Movie: ★★ The Emperor Waltz (musical comedy, 1948) Bing Crosby. (To 3 p.m.) 513032
(SBK) Family Ties
(TBS) (1:05) Movie: ★★ Matlock: The Billionaire (To 3:05 p.m.) 2507544
(TLC) Laurie Cooks Light /Easy
(TNN) Cookin' USA
(V) Innocent Abroad
(WGN) News (CC)
(YTV) Wonder Why? (CC)

1:30

(3)(5)(12) To Be Announced
(7) The Bold and the Beautiful (CC) 57099
(13) Par la Force du Cercle

(29) The Wonder Years (CC)
(47) Wok With Yan
(N) Coast to Coast (CC)
(SBK) Hogan Family
(TLC) New Southern Cooking
(TNN) Country News
(V) Time of Your Life
(YTV) Big Comfy Couch (CC)

2:00

(2)(9)(13) Another World (CC) 43457 23631 20308
(3) It Figures Rpt.
(4)(11)(12) As the World Turns (CC) 38525 25099 16341
(5)(7) One Life to Live (CC) 87815 72983
(6)(41) $40,000 Chain Reaction
(13) Droits de Femmes
(17) Mystery! Devices and Desires (Part 2 of 6) (CC)
(19) Volunteer Board Development (CC)
(25) Les Splendeurs Naturelles d'Europe
(47) Manuela
(AE) Columbo
(SBK) George of the Jungle
(TLC) Amish Cooking
(TMN) Movie: ★★ Wild West (comedy, 1992) Naveen Andrews. (To 3:30 p.m.) 875544
(TNN) Club Dance
(V) James Robison Rpt.
(WGN) Kojak
(YTV) Lamb Chop's Play-Along

2:30

(3) Travel Magazine
(6)(41) Entertainment Desk
(13) Enquete sur les Enfants

Mal-aimes
(19) The Senior Report (CC)
(25) Pourquoi pas l'apres-midi?
(29) Harry and the Hendersons
(SBK) Woody Woodpecker
(TLC) Great Country Inns
(TSN) For the Love of the Game (CC) Rpt.
(V) Life Lessons Rpt.
(YTV) Shining Time Station

3:00

(2) Saved by the Bell (CC)
(3) Urban Peasant
(4)(11)(12) Guiding Light (CC) 4983 30896 38438
(5) Coronation Street 7490
(6)(7)(41) General Hospital 78032 59326 923867
(9) The Bold and the Beautiful 8148
(13) Montel Williams Rpt.
(13) Villages et Visages
(17) Sesame Street (CC)
(19) Pins and Needles
(29) Conan the Adventurer
(47) Incontri See 8:30 p.m.
(AE) Smart!
(MM) FrenchKiss
(N) Canada Live (Live) (CC)
(SBK) Tale Spin (CC)
(TBS) (3:05) Bugs Bunny
(TLC) Yvonne's Cookbook
(TMN) VideoPM
(V) Great Canadian History Series Rpt.
(WGN) Designing Women (CC)
(YTV) Camp Cariboo (CC)

3:30

(2) Family Matters (CC)
(3) Fresh Prince of Bel-Air
(5) The Munsters

(9) The Marriage Counselor (Part 1 of 2)
(13) Mademoiselle
(19) Middle East (CC)
(23) GED (Spanish)
(25) Bino Fabule
(29) Tom & Jerry Kids (CC)
(47) Vivere al 100 per Cento
(57) Canada at War
(AE) Columbo
(FA) Chip 'N Dale's Rescue Rangers (CC)
(MM) RapCity
(SBK) Darkwing Duck (CC)
(TBS) (3:35) Captain Planet and the Planeteers (CC)
(TLC) Biba's Italian Kitchen
(TMN) Movie: ★★ The Sandlot (drama, 1993) Tom Guiry. (To 5:15 p.m.) 4496235
(TSN) Hang Loose Rpt.
(TV5) Nouvelles
(V) Catholic Journal Rpt.
(WGN) The Hallo Spencer Show
(YTV) Samurai Pizza Cats

4:00

(2) Full House (CC)
(3) Mork and Mindy
(4)(57) Oprah Winfrey (CC)
(5) Degrassi Junior High
(6)(41) Saved by the Bell (CC)
(7) Golden Girls (CC)
(9) The Cosby Show (CC)
(11) Matlock (CC)
(12) The Wonder Years (CC)
(13) A Different World (CC)
(13) Mission: Action!
(19) Widget (CC)
(23) Hooked on Aerobics
(25) Anne . . . La Maison aux Pignons Verts
(29) Tiny Toon Adventures

C. Write the names of three programs you would like to see.

Program	Time	Channel
_____	_____	_____
_____	_____	_____
_____	_____	_____

Explain your choices to a partner.

10 More Stories from Toronto

A. Do you like it when friends correct your English? Read how Sagvan feels about it. Do you agree or disagree with him?

I agree ☐   I disagree ☐

because _____ .

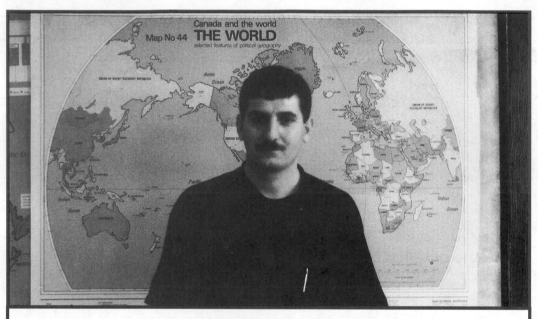

I have two Canadian friends. They help me a lot with English. One of them is a history professor. He has studied a lot about the Kurdish people. He's from England, and he has lived here for about 30 years. I call him, and he calls me, and we talk sometimes.

One day when we were talking, he said to me, "Sorry, but do you want me to tell you when you say something wrong in English?" He was worried that I was going to get angry. But I wasn't angry at all. I told him, "Please correct me when I am wrong."

Now when I talk to him, he is like my teacher. If I talk to someone, and he goes along with everything I say, maybe I will keep on making mistakes. I'm happy when my friend corrects my English.

Sagvan Said is Sadette Cakalli's classmate at Holy Name School in Toronto. He is originally from the Kurdish area of northern Iraq.

B. Read about Curtiss Mollinson's method for learning new vocabulary.
Do you think you will try Curtiss' method?

I probably will try it ❑   I probably won't try it ❑

IDIOMS
back home
make sense

English back home and English here in Canada are totally different. In this country, you have to speak correct English or you won't make any sense. This is the land of opportunity, but you have to read and write well if you want a good job. That's why I came back to school. I don't want to spend my whole life in a kitchen, cooking for $7.00 an hour.

I like to read a lot. Sometimes I just pick up the newspaper or a book. I also like all kinds of magazines. I make a list of all the new words I find. My teacher helps me pronounce the words and find them in a dictionary. I try to remember how to spell them and use them in my own writing.

Curtiss Mollinson is originally from Jamaica. He has lived in Toronto for seven years. He works part-time as a cook at "Mr. Green Jeans" restaurant, and is a full-time student in Laura Negroni's class at the LaSalle Adult Education Program.

C. Which methods for learning English are helpful to you?

	Helpful	Not Helpful
Talking to friends on the telephone.	❑	❑
Asking a friend to correct your English.	❑	❑
Reading the newspaper.	❑	❑
Making a list of all the new words you read.	❑	❑
Looking up new words in a dictionary.	❑	❑

 Tell a partner.

A. Read both stories. Which method do you think is best? Tell a partner.

B. Circle the words you want to remember.

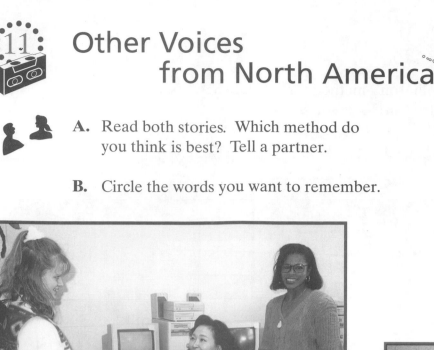

Computers are a big help to students who are learning a second language. I know, because I was an ESL student just a few years ago.

In this center, we have two computers with CD-ROM* drives. Students can use these to get information from dictionaries and atlases. We also have an encyclopedia on CD-ROM. Some other programs help students practice their grammar or improve their writing skills.

I enjoy working here because students feel relaxed here. I like helping them help themselves.

Clarissa Lozano is originally from Colombia. She works in the ESL Resource Center at Bergen Community College in Paramus, NJ. In this photo, she is standing on the right.

I love talk radio. I listen to it all the time. I haven't called in yet. My English isn't good enough. One more year and I'll be ready to call with my opinions.

I like English grammar too. I have many grammar books. I complete one and then start learning from the same book all over again. Each time I pick up something new. There's no end to learning a new language. I'll learn until I die.

Mr. Byung Do Oh studies English at the Korean Center in San Francisco, CA. He is 78 years old.

IDIOM
pick up

*CD-ROM—Compact Disc-Read Only Memory

Bringing the Outside in: Things That Help Us Learn

A. Bring in something that helps you learn or practice English outside the classroom. Show a book, a newspaper, or a magazine you enjoy reading, or play a music tape you like to listen to. Tell the class how it helps you.

B. Bring in the entertainment section and the TV listings from a local newspaper. Choose something to do this weekend that might give you an opportunity to practice your English. Describe it to the class.

Make a list of interesting ideas.

Event	Date	Time
_____	_____	_____
_____	_____	_____
_____	_____	_____

Ideas for Action: Trying New Methods

A. What do you think of Gianpaolo Conti's method for practicing his English?

Every chance I get, I call a toll-free 800 number to get more information about something. It's free, and it helps me practice asking questions and listening to the answers.

Gianpaolo Conti is from Italy. He lives in New York City.

B. Work with a small group of classmates. Look through a magazine or the yellow pages of your telephone book for advertisements about a product or service you want to learn more about. Find advertisements with a telephone number to call for further information. Make sure that the number is local or toll-free (beginning with 1-800).

C. Make a list of the numbers that your group will call.

D. Write two questions you will ask when you call. Practice your questions with the group.

Word Bank

Choose eight new words or expressions from this unit that you want to remember. Use them in sentences of your own.

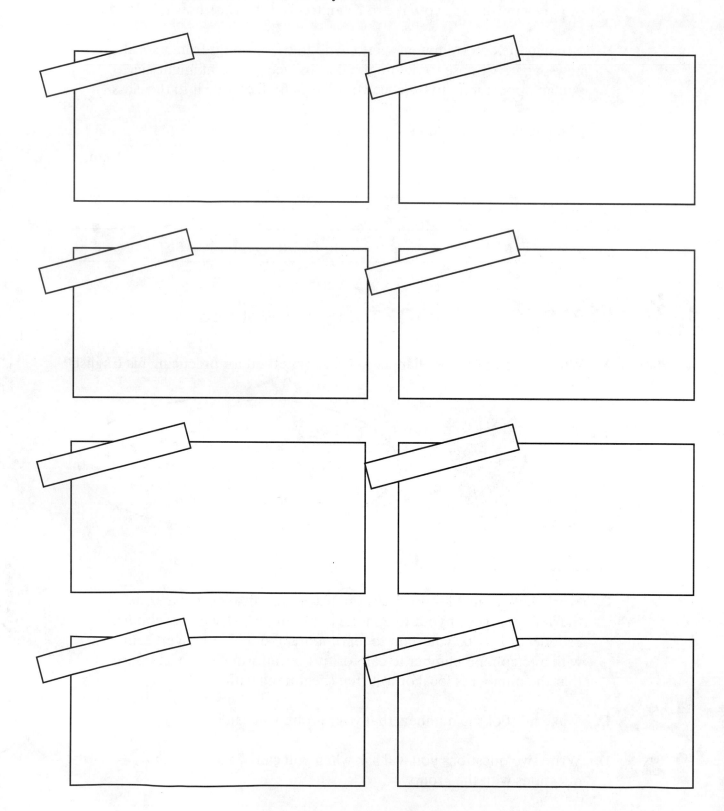

:15: Options for Learning: English Outside the Class

A. How do you want to get more information or practice English outside the classroom? Check (✔) your answers. Add other ideas if you wish.

	Already Do	Want to Learn	Not Interested
Read a schedule of courses	_____	_____	_____
Call for more information about courses or programs	_____	_____	_____
Read ads for movies	_____	_____	_____
Apply for a library card	_____	_____	_____
Other? _____	_____	_____	_____

B. Tell a partner or the class what you already do and what you want to learn to do.

C. Ask your teacher for a *Collaborations* worksheet to work on one of these goals.

:16: Looking Back

Think about your learning. Complete this form. Then tell the class your ideas.

A. The most useful thing I learned in this unit was _____

_____.

B. I would still like to learn _____.

C. I learned the most by working

_____ alone. _____ with a partner. _____ with a group.

D. The activity I liked best was 1 2 3 4 5 6 7 8 9 10 11 12 13 14 15

because _____.

E. The activity I liked least was 1 2 3 4 5 6 7 8 9 10 11 12 13 14 15

because _____.

Checklist for Learning

I. Vocabulary: Check (✔) the words and phrases you know. Add more words and
phrases if you wish. For extra practice, write sentences with the words.

Words for Learning a New Language

_____ understand
_____ speak
_____ listen
_____ read
_____ write
_____ talk
_____ ask
_____ answer
_____ respond

IDIOMS

_____ back home
_____ make sense
_____ pick up

Languages

_____ English
_____ Albanian
_____ Kurdish
_____ Spanish
_____ French
_____ Chinese
_____ Russian
_____ _____
_____ _____

TV Programs

_____ soap operas
_____ news
_____ cartoons
_____ sports
_____ _____
_____ _____

Things to Read

_____ book
_____ newspaper
_____ magazine
_____ program schedule
_____ dictionary
_____ _____
_____ _____

II. Language: Check (✔) what you can do in English. Add more ideas if you wish.

I can

_____ explain my reasons for wanting to join a class or program.
_____ describe what I was doing when something else happened.
_____ evaluate my English language abilities, past and present.
_____ describe how I like to learn a new language.
_____ apologize to a friend.
_____ scan a TV schedule for programs I might like to watch.
_____ explore new ways of learning English.
_____ _____
_____ _____

III. Listening: Listen to the Review Interview at the end of Unit 2. Ask your teacher for
the *Collaborations* worksheet.

Unit 3

Changing Family Roles in San Francisco

The beautiful city of San Francisco, California attracts immigrants from all over the globe, and Asia in particular. In this unit, you will meet Korean and Filipino families who live in the San Francisco area.

San Francisco, CA

Mrs. Lee's Story

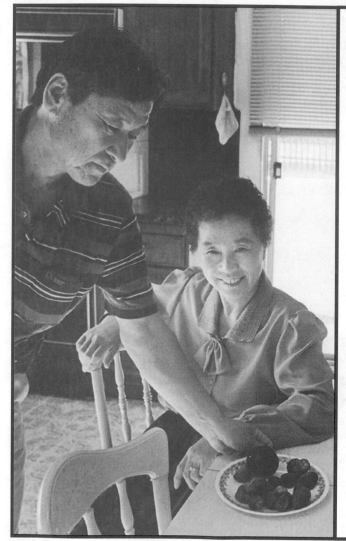

©Ken Light

It has always been my primary responsibility to raise my four children and worry about them. Everything to do with the kids was my job—their education, clothing, and health.

But when I came to this country from Korea in 1979, some things changed for me. In Korea, I used to stay home all the time. Now, I get out of the house. I work, I drive, and I play golf with my girlfriends. I didn't use to have hobbies. But now I'm more like American women.

My husband has changed too. He's more American. He's retired, and he has a lot of time, so he prepares dinner for me. He likes to do this because he likes me. I guess I should say he **loves** me!

In Korea, he used to do nothing around the house. He didn't help me at all—only with babysitting. His Korean friends don't cook. They think he's strange. But he's different from them, and I'm lucky. He cooks, he vacuums, he gardens, and he grows vegetables.

Sam Hwe Lee is from Korea. She works at the Korea Center in San Francisco, CA.

- Who does the cooking in your family?

- Who does the other chores?

- Have your family roles changed in this country?

Playing with Story Language

Follow the steps:

A. Close your eyes and listen to the whole story. Listen again to the second paragraph.

B. Write the words in the correct order in the blanks. Don't look at page 34!

But _____ when I came to _____ this country
I   came   to   when

from Korea in 1979, _____.
things   changed   for   some   me

In Korea, _____
I   stay   used   to   home

all the time. Now, I get out of the house. I work, I drive, and I

_____. I
golf   girlfriends   with   my   play

_____ hobbies. But now
didn't   have   to   use

_____.
more   like   I'm   women   American

C. Work with a partner. Read your sentences to each other. Discuss any differences. Look back at the story to check your answers.

D. With your partner, think of a good title for Mrs. Lee's story on page 34. Write the title below.

_____

Doing It in English: Talking about Changes

A. How have the Lees changed? Look at the sentences about Mrs. Lee.

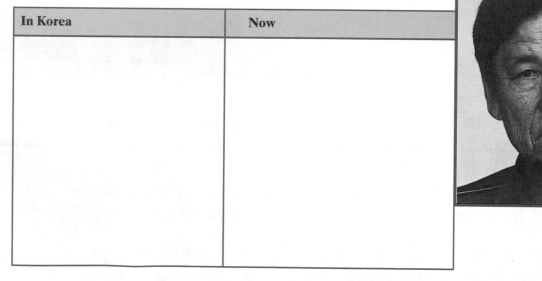

In Korea	Now (In San Francisco)
Mrs. Lee **used to stay** home.	She gets out of the house.
	She works.
She **didn't use to drive.**	She drives.
She **didn't use to have** hobbies.	She plays golf.

Past with *used to*
In Korea, Mrs. Lee **used to stay** home. She **didn't use to drive**.
We can use **used to** to tell about things that happened regularly in the past.

What about Mr. Lee? Write sentences about him.

In Korea	Now

B. Are the Lees like your family?
How? Tell the class.

Then give your opinion. Are the
changes in the Lees' lives good
ones? Why or why not?

Mr. Lee is like my father because...

Mrs. Lee is like my wife because...

Mr. Lee is not like me because...

C. Write about four changes in your life. Tell what you used to do and what you do now.

In My Native Country	Here	Are You Happy about the Changes?		
		YES	**NO**	**NOT SURE**
I used to _____ _____	_____ _____	❑	❑	❑
I used to _____ _____	_____ _____	❑	❑	❑
I didn't use to _____ _____	_____ _____	❑	❑	❑
I didn't use to _____ _____	_____ _____	❑	❑	❑

Tell a partner or small group about the changes. Explain why you are happy or not about each change.

4 Journal Writing

Write about the changes in *your* life. You can write about how family members have changed, too. Tell if the changes are good or bad.

Before you write, look at Mrs. Lee's story on page 34. How many **paragraphs** are there? With the class, discuss **why** she used new paragraphs. In your story, use more than one paragraph if you need to.

More Stories from San Francisco

A. Read the two stories on these pages. Do these families divide the chores the same way your family does? Put a check (✔) next to the parts that remind you of your family.

> **Reading Strategy**
>
> Good readers connect their own experiences with what they read.

I've been married only one year. I do all the cooking myself. In the kitchen, I do all the cleaning up after meals. But my husband cleans the living room, so we share the housework.

Korean wives usually take care of all the money matters in the family. They have to make ends meet. But in our case, my husband does it. He's been in this country much longer than me, and he understands these things.

I think it's easier to be married in the U.S. than in Korea. For Koreans, families matter a lot. A wife has many responsibilities toward her husband's parents. For instance, I call them every day to say, "How are you doing today? How is work going?" I must keep in touch with them. It's my job, not my husband's. My in-laws watch me closely. They watch my abilities. They watch how I spend money. But it would be worse if we all lived in Korea. In-laws there are even more demanding.

Seung Ju Hong attends the City College of San Francisco. She came to the U.S. three years ago. Here, she is calling her in-laws.

> **IDIOMS**
> make ends meet
> keep in touch

Mrs. Lirios: As a wife, I have primary responsibility for the children, my three sons and a daughter. On weekends, I always prepare the menus and food for the whole week. My daughter helps in these chores, but not my sons. I'm the money manager. Women are usually in charge of money in the Philippines. We have to figure out how to make ends meet.

Mr. Lirios: Considering that we both work, I'm not the primary breadwinner. What do I do around the house? I fix the car; I play tennis. If there is housework, I'll help her on the weekends. She does the marketing, but I'm the marketing director. I tell her what to buy.

Mrs. Lirios: In the house, I manage everything, but he is the boss. The male is in charge of disciplining the children in the Philippines. He must set a good example. My husband is always home by 6:00 P.M. He's never late. He doesn't drink. He doesn't go around at night.

Mr. and Mrs. Lirios arrived in San Francisco from the Philippines in 1994. They study at the Filipino Training Center.

B.

Do you agree with these ideas from the stories?	I Agree	I Disagree
1. Women should manage everything in the house.	❑	❑
2. Men must be the boss in the family.	❑	❑
3. Wives should keep in touch with the in-laws.	❑	❑
4. Married men shouldn't go around at night.	❑	❑
5. Mothers should have primary responsibility for the children.	❑	❑
6. Fathers, not mothers, must discipline the children.	❑	❑

Tell the class your opinions.

Doing It in English: Talking about Responsibilities

A. Read more about Mrs. Lee's responsibilities as a mother.

Three of my children are married. I'm still looking for a son-in-law. My daughter is 32. I must find a husband for her. It's my responsibility, and it's our custom. My husband has to look too. I already found husbands for my other daughters. I found them in Korea. I have many friends there who looked around for me.

What must she do? What must her husband do? Do parents in your country have the same responsibility?

B. Write one responsibility of each person on pages 38–39.

Seung Hong must _____.

Mrs. Lirios has to _____.

Mr. Lirios must _____.

Must/Have to		
I You We They } **must** **have to**	discipline the children.	
He } **must** She } **has to**	look for a husband for his daughter. look for a husband for her daughter.	
Use **must** + verb or **have to** + verb to express an obligation or necessity.		

C. What about you?
What are your main responsibilities at home? Write four sentences.

1. ___I must_____

2. ___I have to_____

3. _____

4. _____

Tell a partner.

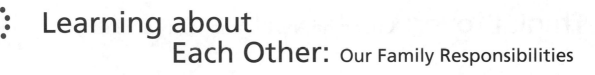

(7) Learning about Each Other: Our Family Responsibilities

A. Who lives in your household? Write their names and their relationship to you *(mother, sister, etc.)* in the boxes next to **ME**.

Who does these chores? For each chore, check (✔) one or more boxes.

	Me			
Cook dinner				
Do the dishes				
Call parents or in-laws				
Manage the money				
Fix the car				
Wash the car				
Clean the kitchen				
Clean the bathroom				
Do the laundry				
Do the grocery shopping				
Take care of young children				
Discipline the children				
Fix things in the house				
Take out the garbage				
Other:				

 B. Work in a small group. Show your chart and tell about work in your household. Is the division of chores fair? Tell why or why not.

I cook, I clean, I do the laundry. I do 90% of the chores.

Is that fair? Is that OK with you?

90% = 90 percent

Think It over: Changing North American Families

A. Look at the large print in the chart below. What information will this chart tell you?

B. Use the chart to complete these sentences.

1. In 1970, U.S. men did _____ hours of housework each week.

2. In 1990, U.S. men worked _____ hours each work at home.

3. In _____ , U.S. women did 8 hours more housework per week than in 1990.

4. In both 1990 and 1970, _____ did more housework.

C. Talk with the class. Give your opinion about the following questions.

1. Why are men in the U.S. doing more housework? Why are women doing less?

2. Are the same changes happening in your native country?

3. In your native country, who does more household chores?

D. Read the two stories about North American families. Are they like families in your country? Why or why not?

Tell a partner and then the class.

I grew up in the U.S. My husband is from Bolivia. We both work full time at demanding jobs. At home, we try to be equal partners—to work together and help each other. Sometimes we argue about who should do work like grocery shopping or straightening the house. But we both do some work in the house, and we both have money responsibilities. Also, we both have always taken care of our daughter since she was a tiny baby.

Roseanne Mendoza is the *Collaborations* editorial director. She lives with her family in Dana Point, CA.

I'm a single mother. I'm raising my baby alone. The best part of being a single mom is my unconditional love for him. The hardest part is the financial responsibility. I am 100% responsible for our housing, food, and other expenses. When I do the household chores, I put him on my back. It's easy now, but I'm afraid of the day he begins to walk.

Virginia Tone lives with her son in Madrid, NM.

Bringing the Outside in: A Family Survey

Take your own survey of North American families.

With the class, decide on the questions you want to ask. With a partner or individually, do one or more interviews. Bring the results to class. With the help of your teacher, you may want to put the results in chart-like form.

These are the questions one class wrote: Who is the boss in your family?
Who does the cooking?
Who takes care of money matters?

10 Ideas for Action: Managing Responsibilities at Home

A. Read the story below. The writer has problems at home. What do you think she should do? What should she say? Write three suggestions with a group.

1. _____ She should _____

2. _____

3. _____

> My problem is that I'm always tired. I live with my husband, our two kids, and my husband's mother. My husband and I both work full time. Every day after work, I pick up my kids (10 and 12 years old) from school. We stop at the supermarket on the way home to do the shopping. While I cook dinner, my husband watches TV, reads the paper, or chats with his mother. Sometimes when dinner isn't ready on time, he gets angry. I get angry too, but I don't say anything.
>
> —Name withheld upon request

B. Tell the class your suggestions. Tell what you think will happen if the woman follows your suggestions.

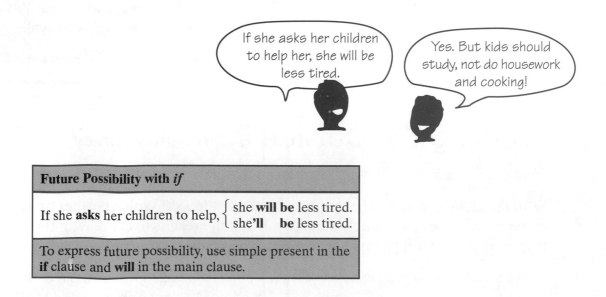

> If she asks her children to help her, she will be less tired.

> Yes. But kids should study, not do housework and cooking!

Future Possibility with *if*	
If she **asks** her children to help,	she **will be** less tired. she **'ll be** less tired.
To express future possibility, use simple present in the **if** clause and **will** in the main clause.	

Other Voices from North America

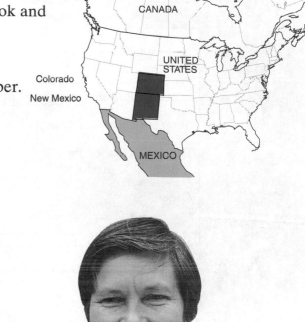

A. Work with a partner. Choose one of the stories to read. After two minutes, close your book and retell the story to your partner.

B. Read the other story.

C. Circle the new words you want to remember.

I have just come to this country, so I don't have much experience with men's and women's roles here.

But I can tell you about men's roles in Macedonia, where I come from. The older generation of men helps out at home sometimes, but they won't admit it to their friends. It would ruin their "macho" image.

Men of my generation are not embarrassed about doing the housework. We sometimes even brag about being so helpful around the house.

Of course, this changes from family to family and from town to town. But you can feel the changes. Slowly but surely, the spirit of equality is entering the minds of all men.

Lazar Dimitrijev is from the former Yugoslav Republic of Macedonia. He lives in Denver, CO.

In my country, wives usually do all the domestic chores. But here husbands share the housework.

In my country, husbands usually think that cooking is a woman's job. They come to the kitchen only to eat. But here I see many husbands who like to cook, and who cook well.

Another big difference between Russian and American families is that American wives are more free. They have real independence. They can go out, they can earn money for themselves, they can change the place they live, and they can easily get divorced.

Rina Martemianova is from Russia. She studies ESL at the University of New Mexico at Los Alamos.

12 Options for Learning: English at Home

A. How do you want to use English at home? Check (✔) your answers.
Add other ideas if you wish.

	Already Do	Want to Learn	Not Interested
Call your child's school	_____	_____	_____
Write a note to your landlord	_____	_____	_____
Shop in the classified ads	_____	_____	_____
Read safety labels on household products	_____	_____	_____
Other? _____	_____	_____	_____
_____	_____	_____	_____

B. Tell a partner or the class what you already do and what you want to learn to do.

C. Ask your teacher for a *Collaborations* worksheet on one of these goals.

13 Looking Back

Think about your learning. Complete this form. Then tell the class your ideas.

A. The most useful thing I learned in this unit was _____

_____.

B. I would still like to learn _____.

_____.

C. I learned the most by working

_____ alone.   _____ with a partner.   _____ with a group.

D. The activity I liked best was   1   2   3   4   5   6   7   8   9   10   11   12

because _____.

E. The activity I liked least was   1   2   3   4   5   6   7   8   9   10   11   12

because _____.

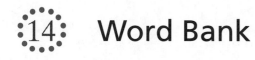

Word Bank

Choose eight new words or expressions from this unit that you want to remember. Use them in sentences of your own.

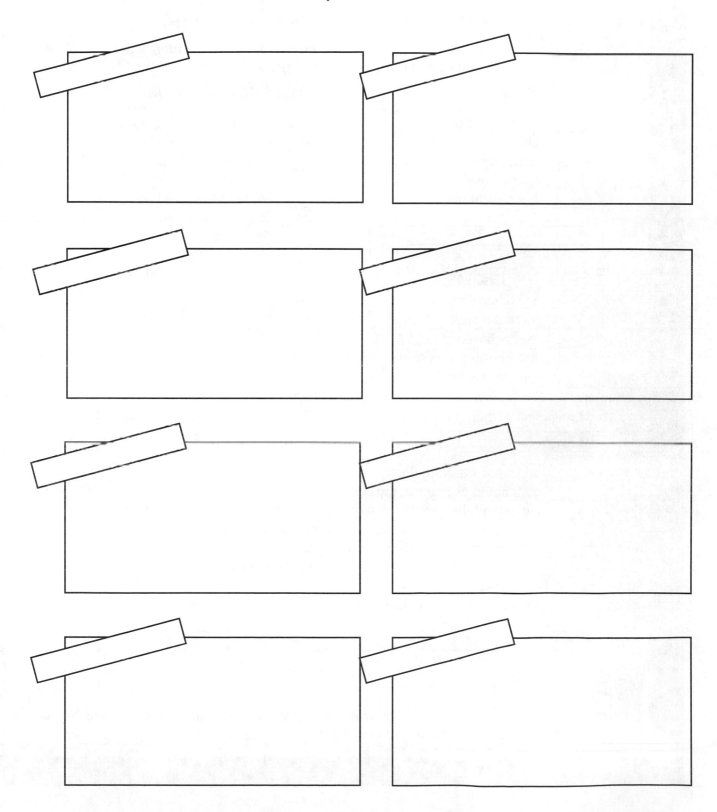

Checklist for Learning

I. Vocabulary: Check (✔) the words and phrases you know. Add more words and phrases if you wish. For extra practice, write sentences with the words.

Work Nouns

_____ responsibility
_____ chore
_____ obligation
_____ housework
_____ housecleaning
_____ _____
_____ _____

IDIOMS

_____ make ends meet
_____ keep in touch
_____ be in charge of
_____ set a good example
_____ the breadwinner

Household Chore Verbs

_____ wash the dishes/do the dishes
_____ garden/do the gardening
_____ vacuum/do the vacuuming
_____ iron/do the ironing
_____ cook/do the cooking
_____ shop/do the shopping
_____ fix the car
_____ manage the money
_____ take care of the children
_____ call the in-laws
_____ do the laundry
_____ discipline the children
_____ _____
_____ _____
_____ _____

II. Language: Check (✔) what you can do in English. Add more ideas if you wish.

I can

_____ tell what I used to do.
_____ talk about changes in my life.
_____ agree and disagree.
_____ tell what my responsibilities are with *must* or *have to.*
_____ talk about different household chores.
_____ tell how North American families are changing.
_____ talk about future possibilities with *if.*
_____ give my opinion about family roles and responsibilities.
_____ _____
_____ _____

III. Listening: Listen to the Review Interview at the end of Unit 3. Ask your teacher for the *Collaborations* worksheet.

Getting the Job You Want: Stories from the Southwest

The stories in this unit come from the Southwest. Many Mexicans and Mexican Americans live in the southwestern states of Texas, New Mexico, and Arizona.

UNITED STATES (ALASKA)

CANADA

UNITED STATES

MEXICO

Southwestern United States

Maria Marcus' Story

Custom Cakes by **Maria**

Weddings • Catering • Special Occasions
484-5561

Maria Marcus

I started my small business here in 1989. I got business cards. I give them to friends and to customers at the supermarket where I work. Mainly, I have been making cakes for friends—for their weddings and birthdays. I love my business, but I still don't get as many orders as I want. I need to advertise in the newspaper.

I have been working at the Southside Supermarket, too, for a year. I quit a catering job before this job because the boss was screaming all the time. I put in lots of applications at businesses near my house. When I applied at the supermarket, they hired me the same day! I had an interview with the manager. She asked, "Have you worked in a supermarket before?" I said, "No, but I have experience making cakes and pastries." She asked me, "Do you have photos of your cakes?" I gave her my business card and went home for my photos. You see, I've been keeping a photo album of every cake I decorate. The manager liked my pictures and hired me for the bakery. After four days, she asked, "Do you want full-time work?" She liked my work and my attitude.

I make $6.50 an hour at the supermarket. This isn't enough for a single mother. In my former job, I was making twice as much. But I prefer to make less money here and not be around a nasty boss.

Maria Marcus lives in El Paso, TX and is from Mexico. She has a small, cake business at home and also works at a supermarket.

- Do you work? How long have you been working at your job?

- Have you had experiences like Maria's?

- Would you like to start a small business?

2 Playing with Story Language

Follow these steps:

A. Close your eyes and listen to the whole story.

B. Complete these sentences from the story. Use the endings in the box below.

1. I started my small business here _____ in 1989. _____

_____

2. I have been working at the Southside Supermarket, too, _____

_____

3. I quit a catering job before this job _____

_____

4. When I applied at the supermarket, _____

_____

5. The manager liked my pictures _____

_____

6. After four days, she asked, _____

_____

7. I prefer to make less money here _____

_____

> because the boss was screaming all the time.
> "Do you want full-time work?"
> for a year.
> and not be around a nasty boss.
> and hired me for the bakery.
> ~~in 1989.~~
> they hired me the same day!

 C. Read your sentences aloud to a partner. Does your partner agree with your answers? Look back at the story if necessary.

Learning about
Each Other: Our Workplaces

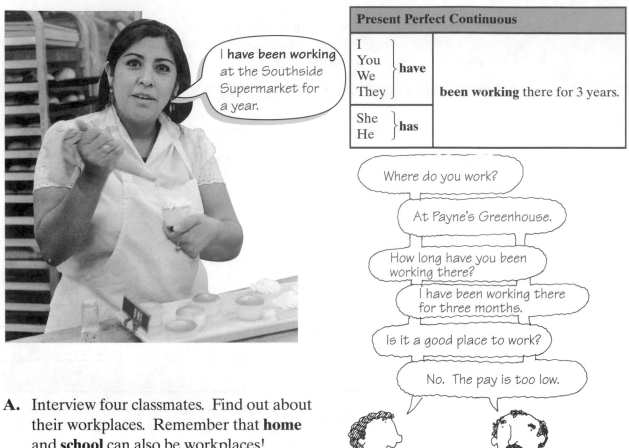

I **have been working** at the Southside Supermarket for a year.

Present Perfect Continuous		
I You We They **have**		**been working** there for 3 years.
She He **has**		

Where do you work?

At Payne's Greenhouse.

How long have you been working there?

I have been working there for three months.

Is it a good place to work?

No. The pay is too low.

A. Interview four classmates. Find out about their workplaces. Remember that **home** and **school** can also be workplaces! (Practice the questions with your class first.)

Classmate's Name	Work Site	How Long?	Good Place to Work?	Why?
1.			YES NO	
2.			YES NO	
3.			YES NO	
4.			YES NO	

B. Discuss what you learned with the class.

C. What do you enjoy doing at work?
What do you dislike doing?
Tell a partner or the class.

I enjoy meeting new people and speaking English at work.

What do you dislike?

I dislike sitting all day.

Gerunds (verb + ing)		Infinitives (to + verb)	
I enjoy	**talking** with coworkers.	*enjoy and dislike **cannot** be used with infinitives*	
I dislike	**doing** physical work.		
I like	**talking** with coworkers.	I like	**to talk** with coworkers.
I don't like	**doing** physical work.	I don't like	**to do** physical work.

(4) Sharing Information: Jobs in the Community

A. What are the most common types of jobs in your community?
Where are they? What do you know about them? With the
class, compare them. Are some better than others?

Learning Strategy

When you pool information with classmates or friends, you can learn a lot. "Two heads are better than one."

Job Title	Job Location(s)	Approximate Pay Rate	How Much English Is Necessary?

B. Which jobs interest you? Ask classmates more about these jobs. Is
anyone in your class looking for a job? Can you help them?

Doing It in English: Telling What's Important in a Job

My job is to sew pockets on blue jeans and other clothes. I like it because I make good money and have good health insurance. It's also enjoyable work. I can talk with my coworkers and the day goes fast. My only problem is with my schedule. It does not give me enough time for my family and home.

Leticia Mowed works at Levi Strauss in El Paso, TX. She studies ESL at El Paso Community College.

IDIOM
make good money

A. Do you remember? What was important to Maria Marcus in a job? What is important to Leticia Mowed, above?

B. What is important to *you* in a job? Check (✔) the three most important things.

1. _____ health insurance
2. _____ good money
3. _____ a good boss
4. _____ good coworkers
5. _____ a clean, healthy work site
6. _____ a flexible work schedule
7. _____ the opportunity to learn things
8. _____ the opportunity for advancement
9. _____ paid sick days
10. _____ paid vacation days
11. _____ a retirement pension
12. _____ enjoyable work
13. _____ (Other) _____
14. _____ (Other) _____

 Tell a partner. Do the two of you agree?

C. Then discuss with the class what you know about **benefits.** Which workplaces in your community have good benefits?

6 Doing It in English: Finding Work

A. Do you remember? How did Maria Marcus find her job at the supermarket? This is how two students at Santa Fe Community College in New Mexico found work.

I take care of children. When I want more baby-sitting jobs, I look at the job notices on the bulletin board at my local library.

I paint houses. I keep an ad in the "Services" section of the local newspaper. A lot of people call me.

B. Interview some classmates who are working or have worked in the past. How did they find work?

Classmate's Name	How He or She Found a Job
_____	_____
_____	_____
_____	_____
	_____

C. Discuss your findings with the class. Did your classmates use any of the following strategies? Which strategies seem the most successful? Check (✔) them.

_____ looking at the "Help Wanted" ads in the newspaper
_____ placing an "Employment Wanted" ad in the newspaper
_____ going to an employment agency
_____ talking to friends
_____ looking on bulletin boards in libraries, supermarkets, etc
_____ calling a business to see if they need someone
_____ starting my own business
_____ using family connections
_____ stopping by an establishment to talk to the boss
_____ sending a resume or letter
_____ filling out an application

More Stories from the Southwest

A. Read both stories. Find one thing you have in common with either Maria or Arturo. Write it here. _____

_____

B. Circle words that are new for you. Can you guess the meaning from the context? Work with the class.

Reading Strategy

Good readers try to understand new words from the context. They don't always go to their dictionaries.

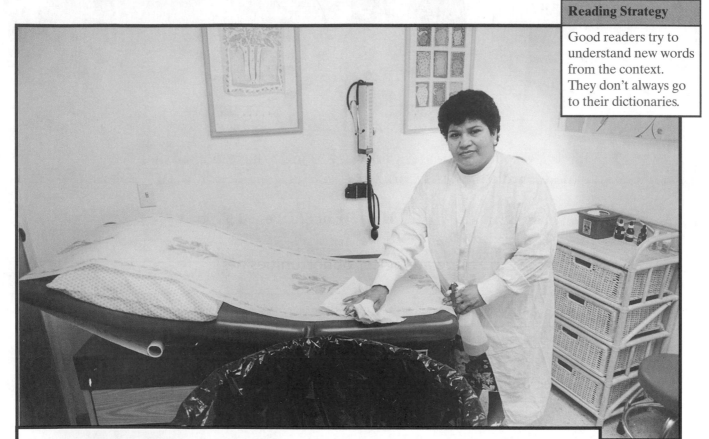

I have been working here at the hospital for eleven years. When I first put in my application, I waited for a year. I kept coming back. I was persistent. The supervisor kept saying, "Oh, you again!" And I said, "I need a job." I called him every week. I kept coming in. I was afraid they would throw away my application. Finally, one day, he telephoned me. He said, "Maria, I need to talk to you." I said, "I'm coming right away," and I got into my car and drove to the hospital. First, I worked only part time, on Saturdays and Sundays. Then he started calling me at odd times. Sometimes I was making tortillas at home and he called. I left my tortillas and came to work. So I was working more and more. I worked part time like this for more than a year before I was offered full-time work.

Maria Medina is a housekeeper in El Paso, TX. She's from Mexico.

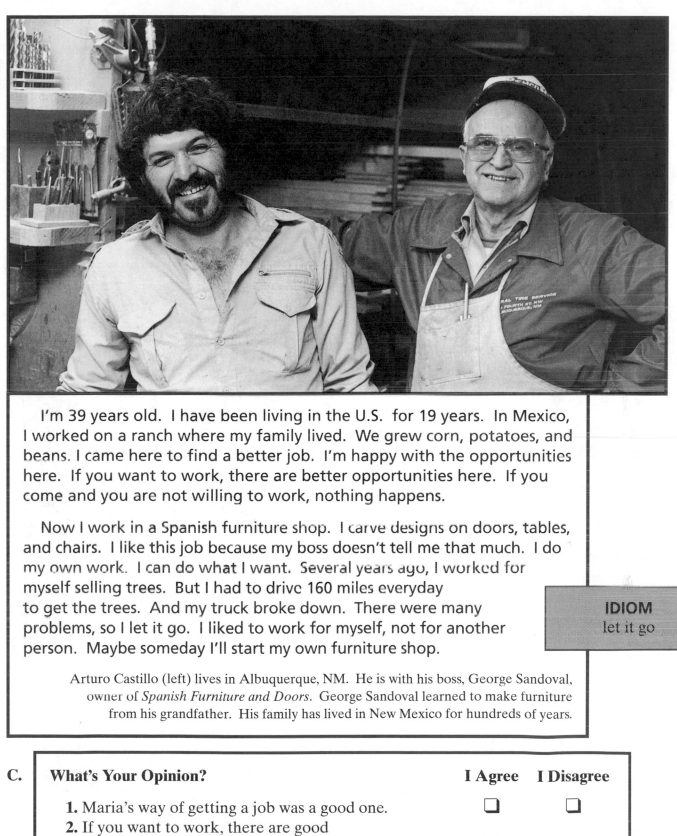

I'm 39 years old. I have been living in the U.S. for 19 years. In Mexico, I worked on a ranch where my family lived. We grew corn, potatoes, and beans. I came here to find a better job. I'm happy with the opportunities here. If you want to work, there are better opportunities here. If you come and you are not willing to work, nothing happens.

Now I work in a Spanish furniture shop. I carve designs on doors, tables, and chairs. I like this job because my boss doesn't tell me that much. I do my own work. I can do what I want. Several years ago, I worked for myself selling trees. But I had to drive 160 miles everyday to get the trees. And my truck broke down. There were many problems, so I let it go. I liked to work for myself, not for another person. Maybe someday I'll start my own furniture shop.

> **IDIOM**
> let it go

Arturo Castillo (left) lives in Albuquerque, NM. He is with his boss, George Sandoval, owner of *Spanish Furniture and Doors*. George Sandoval learned to make furniture from his grandfather. His family has lived in New Mexico for hundreds of years.

C.

What's Your Opinion?	I Agree	I Disagree
1. Maria's way of getting a job was a good one.	❑	❑
2. If you want to work, there are good opportunities in North America.	❑	❑
3. It's better for Arturo to have his own business than to work for another person.	❑	❑

Discuss your opinions with the class.

A. What do employers look for in an employee? What is important to them? Make a list on the board with the class.

B. Read what is important to the three employers below. Which one would you prefer to work for? Why? Tell a partner.

I want nice employees, really nice people. This is my whole life. I work here sixty hours a week, so I want to be around good-natured people. They also have to be honest and motivated. My best workers are immigrants. Many people born in the U.S. don't want to work, but immigrants still have a work ethic.

Bill Reynolds is the owner of Captain Marble in Santa Fe, NM. He cuts and sells large pieces of marble and other stones.

I try to find out if a new employee is interested in learning. That's the most important thing. I hire new employees on a trial basis, for two weeks. I keep them if they are interested in the job and in learning more. My employees must be hard workers. I like them to be on time and reliable too. But these are secondary. Sometimes Arturo is late. I don't like that, but I accept it because he is such a hard worker.

George Sandoval owns a Spanish furniture shop in Albuquerque, NM.

IDIOM
on a trial basis

I have only two employees. One is a receptionist and the other is a dance instructor. I look for friendly employees. My customers won't come back if we're not friendly. Reliability is also important. My last receptionist missed many days of work. I had to fire her.

Victoria Ellis owns an exercise studio in Brooklyn, NY. She is from England.

9   Bringing the Outside In: Guest Speakers

Invite one or two small business owners to your class. Ask them to
explain how they started their businesses. Prepare other questions for
them, too.

10   Journal Writing

Write about your work. You can write
about a boss, a job interview, a day at work,
or your experience looking for work.

To write what you or someone else said, you
can use these forms:

Direct Speech
I *said,* "I have experience making cakes and pastries." She *asked* me, "Do you have photos of your cakes?"
Notice where the commas (,) and quotation marks (" ... ") are placed.

11   Ideas for Action: Starting a Small Business

Think about a small business that *you* could start.

A.   First, write down your abilities and interests.

Talking about Ability
I can + verb I know how + infinitive I'm good at + gerund

Things I Know How to Do

_____

_____

_____

Things I Enjoy Doing

_____

_____

_____

Use your own paper to write more, if you wish.

   B.   Work with a small group. Tell each other about your abilities and
interests. Then, together, brainstorm one possible small business
each of you could start.

Think It Over: Jobs and the Economy

A. Look at the graph below. Read the large print, but cover the rest with your hand. With the class, try to **predict** which jobs are growing fast. Write your **predictions** here.

_____

_____

_____

_____

Reading Strategy
Good readers look at titles or headlines before they read and they try to **predict** what is in the text.

B. Now look at the rest of the text. Were any of your predictions correct?   YES ❑
NO ❑

How many jobs are in the health field? _____

What are the non-health occupations? _____

_____

The New Work Force
10 Fastest Growing Occupations:
1990 to 2005

Home health aides
Systems analysts / computer scientists
Personal and home care aides
Medical assistants
Human services workers
X-ray technicians
Medical secretaries
Psychologists
Travel agents
Police officers

0   25   50   75   100
Percent Increase

Source: United States Bureau of the Census

C. Brainstorm these questions with the class. Give your opinions and ideas.

Why are these jobs growing?
Which jobs are becoming less common in North America?

Learning Strategy
Brainstorming with a group is a technique to solve problems. Everyone contributes ideas in a quick, spontaneous way.

13 Other Voices from North America

A. Work with a partner. Choose one of the stories to read. After two minutes, close your book and retell the story to your partner.

B. Read the other story.

C. Circle the new words you want to remember.

I was trained in Pakistan as an engineer. I completed studies in both electrical and mechanical engineering at the University of Pakistan in 1969. I worked there five years. When I arrived in Canada in 1974 with just a few dollars in my pocket, I hoped to get a good job. I applied to many companies, but they all told me, "If you don't have any Canadian experience, forget it!" They think that because we are from the third world, our education is not up to their standard. So I decided to borrow some money and open this clothes shop.

Khaliq Abdul is from Pakistan. He owns a shop in Kensington Market, Toronto, Ontario.

In 1980, when I was tired of my old job, I decided to try to change my career. At that moment, my old friend Sue was looking for a partner. She wanted to open a small shop with toys and stationery. So I joined her and became a shopkeeper.

At first, it was a hard job for me because I had no experience with sales. We ordered our merchandise from vendors and decorated the shop. We put the goods on the shelves, and stuck the price labels on.

After everything was ready, we chose a day to celebrate our grand opening. We sent an advertisement to people living near our shop. The first day we gave a discount to the customers, and we made a lot of money!

Chan Wong So San studies ESL at LaGuardia Community College in New York City. She's from China.

Options for Learning: English at Work

A. How do you want to use English at work? Check (✔) your answers.
Add other ideas if you wish.

	Already Do	Want to Learn	Not Interested
Understand paychecks	_____	_____	_____
Understand work schedules	_____	_____	_____
Write a thank-you note to an interviewer	_____	_____	_____
Design a business card	_____	_____	_____
Other? _____	_____	_____	_____

B. Tell a partner or the class what you already do and what you want to learn to do.

C. Ask your teacher for a *Collaborations* worksheet on one of these goals.

Looking Back

Think about your learning. Complete this form. Then tell the class your ideas.

A. The most useful thing I learned in this unit was _____

_____.

B. I would still like to learn _____.

C. I learned the most by working

_____ alone.   _____ with a partner.   _____ with a group.

D. The activity I liked best was 1 2 3 4 5 6 7 8 9 10 11 12 13 14

because _____.

E. The activity I liked least was 1 2 3 4 5 6 7 8 9 10 11 12 13 14

because _____.

Word Bank

Choose eight new words or expressions from this unit that you want to remember. Use them in sentences of your own.

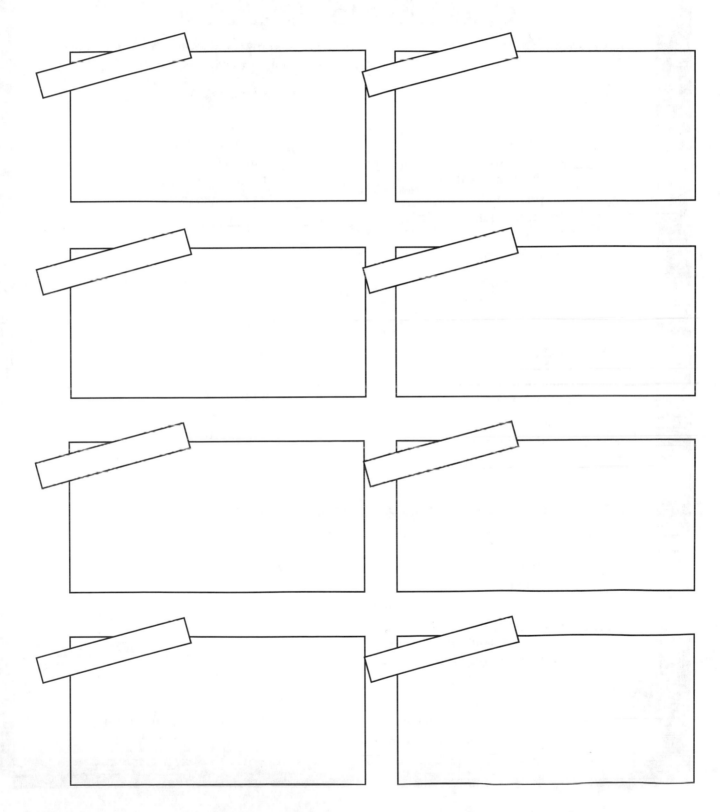

Checklist for Learning

I. Vocabulary: Check (✔) the words and phrases you know. Add more words and phrases if you wish. For extra practice, write sentences with the words.

Job Titles

_____ police officer
_____ engineer
_____ dance instructor
_____ medical assistant
_____ travel agent
_____ furniture maker
_____ business owner
_____ housekeeper

_____ _____
_____ _____
_____ _____

Ways to Find Jobs

_____ look at bulletin boards
_____ go to employment agency
_____ talk to friends
_____ fill out applications
_____ call businesses

_____ _____
_____ _____
_____ _____
_____ _____
_____ _____

Job Benefits

_____ health insurance
_____ paid sick days
_____ retirement pension
_____ paid vacation days

_____ _____
_____ _____

IDIOMS

_____ make good money
_____ let it go
_____ on a trial basis
_____ have in common

II. Language: Check (✔) what you can do in English. Add more ideas if you wish.

I can

_____ tell where I work and how long I have been working there.
_____ tell what is important to _me_ in a job.
_____ list some strategies for finding work.
_____ try to guess new words from context.
_____ write what someone said in direct speech.
_____ talk about my abilities and interests.

III. Listening: Listen to the Review Interview at the end of Unit 4. Ask your teacher for the _Collaborations_ worksheet.

Unit 5
New Lives, New Challenges
in New York City

Most of the stories in this unit are from Brooklyn, New York. Brooklyn is part of New York City, the largest city in North America. Every year, more than 100,000 new immigrants come to live and work in New York City.

New York City

1 The El-Asmar Family Story

When we first arrived in Brooklyn, the only words we could say in English were "yes" and "no." Our children learned English first—it's easier for them, you know. Then they helped us open this store. We've been in business for about five years now.

We have to work twelve hours a day, even on the weekends. If one of us is sick, the others work twice as hard. Of course, we've had to face some problems, but we're doing all right now. Thank God, we can't complain.

IDIOM
we can't complain

We import coffee, spices, dried fruits, nuts, and all kinds of Middle Eastern specialities. This is a really mixed neighborhood, so our customers are from all over the place. Almost nobody who walks in the door was born here in Brooklyn. Most of our customers are Yemenis and Lebanese, but we also get Moroccans, Spanish Jews, and even a few Chinese people. They use some of the same spices in their cooking.

It's important to be honest and friendly. Some people come here just to talk. Maybe they buy a little bit of coffee or a few nuts. Then they stay and talk for hours. That's OK with us. We don't rush them. We want people to feel at home here.

Asa'ad El-Asmar immigrated from Lebanon with his family twelve years ago. "El-Asmar International Delights," his family's store, is located on Atlantic Avenue in Brooklyn.

- What kind of neighborhood do you live in?
- Where are most of your friends and neighbors from?
- Where do you feel "at home" in your neighborhood?

2 Playing with Story Language

Follow these steps:

A. Close your eyes and listen to the whole story.

B. Complete these sentences from the story. Use the endings in the box below.

1. When we first arrived in Brooklyn, _____

_____

2. We've been in business _____

_____

3. We have to work twelve hours a day, _____

_____

4. If one of us is sick, _____

_____

5. Of course, we've had to face some problems, _____

_____

6. We import coffee, spices, dried fruits, nuts, _____

_____

7. This is a really mixed neighborhood, _____

_____

8. Almost nobody who walks in the door _____

_____

was born here in Brooklyn.	and all kinds of Middle Eastern specialties.
the others work twice as hard.	so our customers are from all over the place.
for about five years now.	the only words we could say in English were "yes" and "no."
but we're doing all right now.	even on the weekends.

C. Read your sentences aloud to a partner. Does your partner agree with your answers? Look back at the story if necessary.

Doing It in English: Telling about Favorite Places

Some people come here just to talk. Maybe they buy a little coffee or a few nuts. Then they stay and talk for hours.

A. Where do you spend your free time? Where do you go to get the things you need? List four of your favorite places. Write your main purpose for going to each place. Use **to** or **for**.

Phrases of Purpose
Some people come here **to talk.**   Some people come here **for conversation.**
Use *to* with a verb or *for* with a noun to explain your purpose for doing something.

Place	Near or Far?	Purpose
_____	_____	_____
_____	_____	_____
_____	_____	_____
_____	_____	_____

B. Tell a partner about each place.

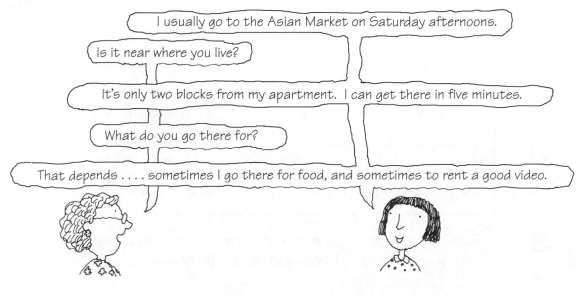

I usually go to the Asian Market on Saturday afternoons.

Is it near where you live?

It's only two blocks from my apartment. I can get there in five minutes.

What do you go there for?

That depends . . . . sometimes I go there for food, and sometimes to rent a good video.

Learning about Each Other: Our Shopping Habits

A. Do you remember some of the things you can buy at El-Asmar International Delights? Look back at the story and make a list here. Add some other things that you think might be in the store.

Can I help you?

Rose El-Asmar helps customers find what they want at El-Asmar International Delights. She has learned English on the job, and from her children.

_____

_____

_____

_____

_____

_____

 B. Work with a partner. Roleplay a conversation between Rose and a customer. Practice asking for the amounts you want.

I'd like a pound of Turkish coffee.

Anything else?

Amounts
an **ounce** of curry powder
a **pound** of coffee
a **box** of cereal
a **package** of dates
a **jar** of jam
a **bottle** of milk

C. Work in a small group. Find out about each other's shopping habits.

Classmate's Name	Favorite Place to Shop for Food	Why?	Two Foods and the Exact Amounts He or She Usually Buys.

Think It Over: Immigrant Communities Past and Present

A. Look at the photograph and read the description.

> Between 1870 and 1900, more than eleven million people came to live in North America. Many of them settled in large cities. This picture shows a neighborhood in New York City where many new immigrants from Europe lived about 100 years ago. Living conditions were poor, and there were very few places for adults to learn English.

Reading Strategy

When you read about the past, look for exact details about the time and place.

B. Use details from the description to complete each of these sentences.

1. Eleven million immigrants came to North America between

_____ and _____ .

2. In the neighborhood in the photo, many new immigrants came from _____ .

3. This photo shows an immigrant neighborhood in _____
about 100 years ago.

C. How is the neighborhood in the photograph similar to or different from the place you now live?

New York Neighborhood in 1900	Your Neighborhood in the 1990s	
	Similar	Different
Most of the people were immigrants.	❑	❑
People had to work very hard to make a living.	❑	❑
You could buy and sell a lot of things on the street.	❑	❑
Living conditions were crowded and poor.	❑	❑
There were very few places for adults to learn English.	❑	❑

How is your neighborhood similar or different? Tell a partner.

Doing It in English: Describing Neighbors

Learning Strategy

Sharing ideas with classmates helps everyone understand different points of view.

A. Discuss the people in this photograph with a small group of your classmates. Make some guesses. Where are the people from? What languages do they speak? Where do they live? Share your ideas with the group.

B. Think about the people in your neighborhood. Make some general statements to the group. Use some of the words in the box if you wish.

All Most A lot Some A few Not many	of the people in my neighborhood	live in apartments. don't like foreigners. speak Spanish. are immigrants. have good jobs. use drugs.

100% — 50% — 0%

C. With your group, complete these statements about your classmates.

1. All of us   are studying English.

2. Most of us _____

3. A lot of us _____

4. Some of us _____

5. A few of us _____

6. Not many of us _____

Read your sentences to the class.

• • •

A. Read the stories on these two pages.
Read first for the general idea in each story.
Which story was most interesting? Why?

B. Read the stories again. Write one problem
each person has.

Saad: _____

Hilal: _____

> **Reading Strategy**
>
> When you read a story the first time, look for the main idea. Read it again to find specific details and examples.

IDIOMS
hang out
count on

I like working here at the National Association of Yemeni Immigrants. Yemenis come here for many reasons. If they are new in this country, they might need a job, a place to stay, or medical help. All those things are much easier in my country. Some people come to meet friends, eat Yemeni food, or talk about their problems. Others just come to hang out and play cards.

Living in Brooklyn has a lot of advantages. There are a lot of people I can count on if I need help. We also have two mosques right here in this neighborhood, and it is easy to get Arabic newspapers.

As I see it, living here has only one big disadvantage. I don't have any American friends, so my English is not getting much better. Most of the time, I speak Arabic. The only place I speak English is in my ESL class. You know what they say, "If you don't use it, you lose it!"

Saad Al-Montasar is from Yemen. He has
lived in Brooklyn for almost two years.
He studies ESL at Long Island
University, Brooklyn campus.

Crime is not such a big problem in this neighborhood, like it is in other parts of New York City. The main problems for people just arriving from Yemen are finding a job and a place to live.

After they have been here for a while, a lot of Yemeni immigrants have to face different kinds of problems. For example, it's really difficult to raise a family here, because the kids pick up American values at school. They start to forget where they come from.

Another problem is that Americans don't understand much about us. In the media, the only time you see the word, "Arab" is when there is a bombing or something like that. A lot of them think all of us are terrorists, or that we all ride on camels. That makes it hard to make new friends or get a good job. That's why we have to stick together and help each other out.

Hilal Lashuel has lived and worked in Brooklyn for seven years. He studied ESL at Long Island University, where he now studies computer science.

IDIOMS
pick up
stick together

C. Compare the situation in Saad and Hilal's neighborhood to the situation in your community.

	Same in your community?	
	YES	**NO**
We speak our own language most of the time.	☐	☐
There are a lot of people we can count on.	☐	☐
It's hard to find a good job.	☐	☐
It's really difficult to raise a family.	☐	☐
Americans don't understand much about us.	☐	☐

 Share your answers with a partner.

Sharing Information: Your Community

A. Look at the information in this chart about the Atlantic Avenue neighborhood in Brooklyn. In the bottom part, write what you know about *your* neighborhood or town.

Town, Area, or Neighborhood	Languages Spoken	Other Information
Atlantic Avenue area of Brooklyn, New York	• English • Arabic • Spanish • Hebrew • Greek	• a lot of restaurants, food stores, and other small businesses • many large apartment buildings • two mosques, five churches, one temple • three schools • one hospital

B. Work with a small group. Tell your group about your neighborhood. Also, tell what you like and dislike about it.

C. Do you remember what Saad Al-Montasar said about living near other Yemenis? What were the advantages? What was the one big disadvantage? With your group, make a list of the advantages and disadvantages of living near other immigrants from your country.

Advantages (+)

They can help you.

_____

_____

_____

Disadvantages (−)

_____

_____

_____

9 Doing It in English: Comparing Neighborhoods

Brooklyn is a lot **more crowded** than Sanaa.

Saad Al-Montasar used to live in Sanaa, the capital of Yemen. He now lives and studies in Brooklyn, NY.

A. Compare the city, town, or neighborhood where you now live to a place you used to live. Check the boxes next to each description.

Place you live now: _____ = A

Place you used to live: _____ = B

Compare A and B. Which place is . . .	A	B	No Difference
more crowded?	☐	☐	☐
noisier?	☐	☐	☐
more expensive?	☐	☐	☐
more beautiful?	☐	☐	☐
safer?	☐	☐	☐
more exciting?	☐	☐	☐
more modern?	☐	☐	☐
friendlier?	☐	☐	☐
more peaceful?	☐	☐	☐

Comparative Adjectives

Miami is **bigger** than Santo Domingo. Santo Domingo is **more peaceful** and **cheaper.**

To form comparative adjectives, add -er to short adjectives Use *more* with most longer adjectives.

B. Write three sentences that compare these two places. Use the comparative adjectives in the list or try some of your own.

1. _____

2. _____

3. _____

C. Read your sentences aloud to a partner. Tell your partner more about the place where you used to live and the place where you live now.

Think It Over: Problems in Your Community

A. Think about a problem you had when you first arrived in North America. Write a sentence about it.

My biggest problem was _____

Read your sentence aloud to a partner. Explain more about the problem and how you solved it. Where did you go? What did you do?

B. Think about the problems in your community now. Check (✔) the sentences that are true for most people in your community. Add more sentences of your own.

_____ There's a lot of crime; it's not safe to live here.
_____ Nobody has time to talk.
_____ We don't feel at home here.
_____ It's difficult to raise a family .
_____ We can't afford good places to live.
_____ Some people discriminate against us.

_____ _____
_____ _____

_____ _____

C. On page 73, Hilal Lashuel complains that North Americans do not understand much about his country or his culture.

A lot of them think all of us are terrorists, or that we all ride on camels.

Hilal Lashuel is from Yemen. He studies computer science in Brooklyn, NY.

What stereotypes* do some North Americans have about people from your country? What do you tell them? Complete these sentences, and then explain to the class.

They think _____
They say _____

*A **stereotype** is an idea about a group of people that is often wrong because it is not based on enough facts.

Journal Writing

Think about how you would describe the place you now live to a person who has just arrived. In your journal, describe the best things and the worst things about life in your community. Give the newcomer some friendly advice on how to deal with a major problem.

Ideas for Action: Solving Community Problems

 A. With a small group, decide on one community problem that concerns everyone in the group. Write the problem in the circle.

Causes	**Problem**	**Our Solution**

B. Share ideas about causes of the problem. Write them on the lines at the left.

C. Suggest possible solutions to the problem. Write the best ideas in the box at the right. Present your group's ideas to the class.

Bringing the Outside in: Community Media

Bring in a community newspaper, magazine, or newsletter written in English or in your native language. Choose one photograph, advertisement, or article to show the class. Explain to the class why this publication is important to people in your community.

Devika Rani Roerich, the legendary queen of Indian films,

Other Voices from North America

A. Work with a partner. Choose one of the stories to read. After two minutes, close your book and retell the story to your partner.

B. Read the other story.

C. Circle the words you want to remember.

| IDIOM |
| carry things |

Ninety-eight percent of our customers are Vietnamese. This whole shopping center is Vietnamese and Chinese, Chinese from Vietnam. People from Taiwan and Hong Kong are the owners of this place. The Chinese merchants here do a lot of business with Taiwan and Hong Kong. They import their merchandise.

In my store we mainly sell things that were made in the United States, things that our people send back home, like dry goods, vitamins, and medicine for which you don't need a prescription—things they can't get in Vietnam. And because Vietnamese people like French imports—perfumes and clothing—we carry those too.

Here in Westminster we are lucky to live among Vietnamese people. We can almost forget that we are not home.

Huong Nguyen is from Vietnam. Her family's store is in Westminster, CA.

This is the center for immigrants. We can get all kinds of useful information and help here. You know, the customs here are so different, and we need help adjusting to them. We have very good services for seniors.

Older men and women want to know the news, but they can't understand English. They come here to meet friends and exchange the news. They can watch Korean language TV and radio.

We help people solve all kinds of problems: housing problems, medical problems, and social security problems. We have English classes, citizenship classes, Tai Kwon Do classes, and even Korean language classes for young children. We don't want them to forget our language!

John E. Hong is the former president of the Korean Community Center in San Francisco, CA. He is the second from the left in this photograph.

Word Bank

Choose eight new words or expressions from this unit that you want to remember. Use them in sentences of your own.

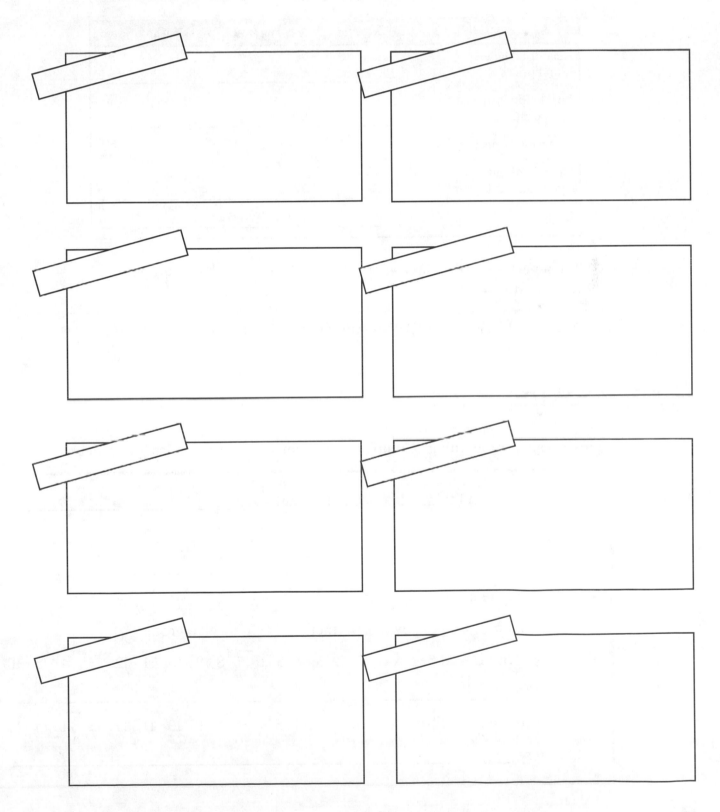

:16: Options for Learning: English in the Community

A. How do you want to get more information or practice English in your community? Check (✔) your answers. Add other ideas if you wish.

	Already Do	Want to Learn	Not Interested
Read food labels and prices	_____	_____	_____
Locate foods in a supermarket	_____	_____	_____
Use public transportation	_____	_____	_____
Find out about apartments for rent	_____	_____	_____
Other? _____	_____	_____	_____

B. Tell a partner or the class what you already do and what you want to learn to do.

C. Ask your teacher for a *Collaborations* worksheet to work on one of these goals.

:17: Looking Back

Think about your learning. Complete this form. Then tell the class your ideas.

A. The most useful thing I learned in this unit was _____

_____.

B. I would still like to learn _____.

C. I learned the most by working

_____ alone.   _____ with a partner.   _____ with a group.

D. The activity I liked best was 1 2 3 4 5 6 7 8 9 10 11 12 13 14 15 16

because _____.

E. The activity I liked least was 1 2 3 4 5 6 7 8 9 10 11 12 13 14 15 16

because _____.

Checklist for Learning

I. Vocabulary: Check (✔) the words and phrases you know. Add more words and phrases if you wish. For extra practice, write sentences with the words and phrases.

Places to Live

_____ city
_____ town
_____ suburb
_____ neighborhood

_____ _____
_____ _____

Words that Describe a Community

_____ large
_____ small
_____ safe
_____ dangerous
_____ mixed
_____ crowded
_____ poor

_____ _____
_____ _____

IDIOMS

_____ on the job
_____ we can't
_____ complain
_____ hang out
_____ can count on
_____ pick up
_____ stick together
_____ carry items in a store

Places to Shop

_____ store
_____ shop
_____ supermarket
_____ mall
_____ market

_____ _____
_____ _____

Food and Drink

_____ tea
_____ spices
_____ fruit
_____ nuts
_____ cheese
_____ bread
_____ rice

_____ _____
_____ _____

II. Language: Check (✔) what you can do in English. Add more ideas if you wish.

I can

_____ describe places to go in my community.
_____ explain my purpose in going somewhere.
_____ ask for specific quantities of food.
_____ describe the people who live in my community.
_____ identify and discuss community problems.
_____ compare different places to live.
_____ read for general ideas and specific examples.

_____ _____
_____ _____

III. Listening: Listen to the Review Interview at the end of Unit 5. Ask your teacher for the *Collaborations* worksheet.

Coming to **North America:**
Stories from Massachusetts

The stories in this unit come from Lowell, MA.
Many immigrants from Southeast Asia (Cambodia,
Laos, and Vietnam) live there.

Massachusetts

John Nguyen's Story

In 1979, John and his older brother escaped from Vietnam in a small fishing boat. Late at night, sixty-five men, women, and children met on the shore and swam one mile to the boat. The younger children were on small rafts, and the adults pushed them. Each person paid the boat owner one bar of gold.

After they traveled seven days and nights in rough waters, without food, they landed in the Philippines. John recalls, "When a boy on the boat died from starvation, I wanted the boat to sink. I wanted to die. I was so afraid."

John Nguyen lives in Lowell, MA. Here, he is at home with his fiancee.

• Was your trip to North America like John's?

Playing with Story Language

Follow these steps:

A. Listen to the story.

B. Match the past verb forms from the story with their base forms.

Past Form	Base Form
swam	meet
died	pay
traveled	swim
escaped	die
wanted	travel
paid	want
met	push
landed	escape
pushed	land

C. Now fill in the blanks with the past verb forms.

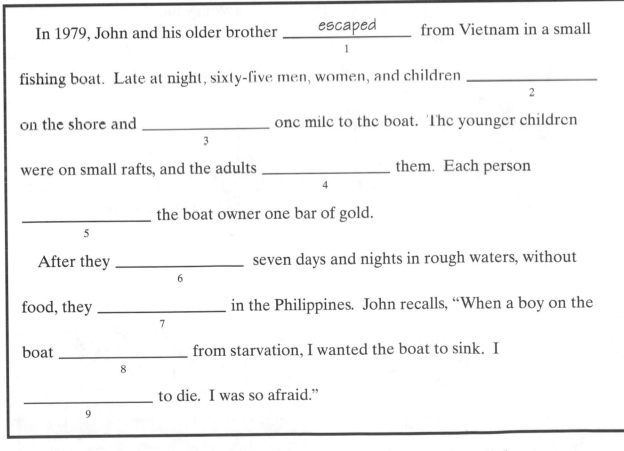

In 1979, John and his older brother _____escaped_____ from Vietnam in a small
                                            1

fishing boat. Late at night, sixty-five men, women, and children _____
                                                                          2

on the shore and _____ one mile to the boat. The younger children
                        3

were on small rafts, and the adults _____ them. Each person
                                            4

_____ the boat owner one bar of gold.
       5

   After they _____ seven days and nights in rough waters, without
                      6

food, they _____ in the Philippines. John recalls, "When a boy on the
                   7

boat _____ from starvation, I wanted the boat to sink. I
             8

_____ to die. I was so afraid."
       9

D. Read the story once to a partner. Then close your book and retell the story.

Learning about Each Other: Our Trips Here

A. Think about *your* trip to North America. Write notes about the trip on the left side of the chart.

B. Work with a partner. Listen to the story of your partner's trip. Take notes on the right side of the chart. Ask questions when you don't understand or when you want further information.

> What do you mean?
> Can you explain that?

> Did you say 1990?

Notes on My Trip to North America	Notes on My Partner's Trip to North America
From where?	**From where?**
When?	**When?**
With whom?	**With whom?**
How? (circle one or more) car truck train bus plane helicopter rowboat raft fishing boat ocean liner (other: _____)	**How?** (circle one or more) car truck train bus plane helicopter rowboat raft fishing boat ocean liner (other: _____)
Other information:	**Other information:**

C. At the end of your story, summarize your trip in one sentence. For example, you can use a sentence beginning with **what**, as in the box.

Explanatory Sentences		
What	a dangerous a scary a long a happy an exciting an awful	trip it was!

4 Journal Writing

A. In your journal, write about your trip to North America. Before you write, make some notes below to remember the events of your trip. Put the events in **chronological order** (the first event, the second event, and so on).

```
_____

1. _____

2. _____

_____

_____

_____

_____
```

B. When you write your story, you can connect two sentences with *after, when,* or *before.* These words show the time relationship between two events.

Look back at John Nguyen's story on page 84. Underline *after* and *when.* Look at the way these words are used.

Tell the class about two events in your trip. Connect the two ideas with *after, when,* or *before.*

When, Before, After		
When I got on the plane, I cried.	OR	I cried *when* I got on the plane.
Before I left, I sold my house.	OR	I sold my house *before* I left.
After I arrived, I called my family.	OR	I called my family *after* I arrived.

Think It Over: Immigration and Global Issues

A. Look at the **title** in the box below. What information will the map give you?

B. Find answers to these questions.

1. How many legal immigrants came to the

U.S. and Canada in 1991? _____

2. Which state or province got the most

immigrants? _____

3. Does the map tell how many people came to

your state or province?   **YES**   **NO**

If yes, how many? _____

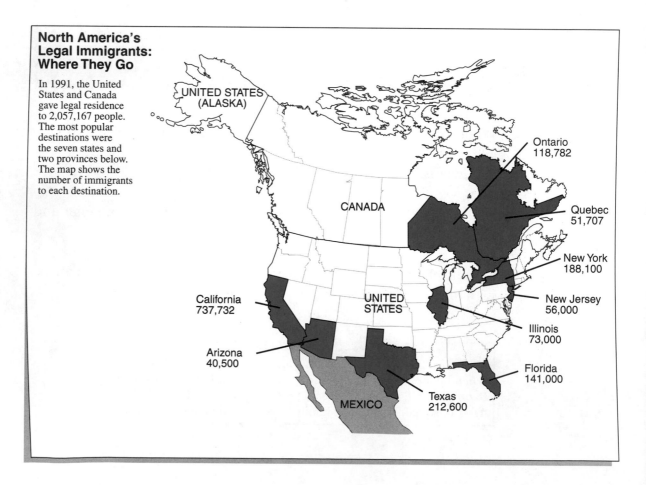

North America's Legal Immigrants: Where They Go

In 1991, the United States and Canada gave legal residence to 2,057,167 people. The most popular destinations were the seven states and two provinces below. The map shows the number of immigrants to each destination.

UNITED STATES (ALASKA)

CANADA

UNITED STATES

MEXICO

Ontario 118,782

Quebec 51,707

New York 188,100

New Jersey 56,000

Illinois 73,000

Florida 141,000

Texas 212,600

Arizona 40,500

California 737,732

C. Why do so many people immigrate each year to North America? Walk around your classroom. Take a survey of your classmates to find out why they came. On a separate sheet of paper, make a chart like this one.

Classmates' Names	Reasons for coming to the United States and Canada

©Ken Light

To the Promised Land

Why did you come to the United States and Canada?

I came because I wanted a better job.

I came because I wanted to help my Children.

Giving reasons with *because*

I immigrated **because** I could not speak freely.
Because I could not speak freely, I immigrated.

Because combines two sentences. It can come in the middle or at the beginning of the sentence. The second way is more common in writing than in speaking.

D. In a small group, look at your results and discuss these questions:

1. Among your classmates, what is the most common reason for immigrating?

2. Can you categorize the reasons into two or more groups?

Learning Strategy

When you *categorize* things, you put similar things together. Categorizing helps you organize information.

6 More Stories from Massachusetts

A. Read both stories. Find one thing you have in common with either Khanh Nguyen or Soeung Chea. Write it here. _____

B. Now circle words that are new for you. Can you guess the meaning from the context? Work with the class.

Khanh Nguyen's brother and sister escaped from Vietnam in 1979. Three years later, they arranged for him and his parents to come. Khanh enrolled in the College of Music at the University of Lowell.

"When I first came here, I was very lonely and blue. It wasn't easy for me to make friends. At my first performance before the school, I walked onto the stage and then turned around and walked back off again. I failed because I was too nervous. I could not cope."

> **IDIOM**
> be blue

A month later, Khanh Nguyen performed his own work before the school. He received three standing ovations.

Khanh Nguyen is from Vietnam. He lives in Lowell, MA.

When I got the news that we could immigrate to the United States, I was very excited. My only hope for life in the U.S. was that there would be no more war—no more shelling and bombing. I just wanted to live in a peaceful place.

Before I came, I was a little worried about living here. I worried about the language and the food. At the refugee camp in the Philippines, I tried to learn some English for six months, but I couldn't remember much. I had never tasted American food. I didn't feel anything when I first arrived. I just hoped that my life would get better. I still don't speak much English, but I can get along without it, and I don't have to eat American food. I shop at Asian food stores and cook only Cambodian food.

Life here is much better than in my country. People can make a living. I want to stay. My grandchildren are Americans. They will succeed here.

Soeung Chea lives in Northampton, MA. She arrived in the U.S. from Cambodia in 1982.

IDIOM
making a living

C. Compare your own situation and experiences with those of Khanh Nguyen and Soeung Chea.

	Same For You?	
	YES	**NO**
Khanh Nguyen escaped from his country.	❑	❑
He was lonely and blue at first.	❑	❑
Soeung Chea was worried about living in the U.S.	❑	❑
She doesn't eat American food.	❑	❑
She believes life is better here.	❑	❑
She wants to stay.	❑	❑

Tell the class.

7 Doing It
in English: Expressing Opinions about North America

A. Read Donna Lee's opinion. Do you agree with her?

America: Land of Opportunity?
  I don't think America is a land of opportunity, especially for the immigrant who doesn't speak English well. I know many people who work in restaurants or in garment factories. They labor very long hours every day, and they don't make much money due to their poor English. Some of these people do the same job year after year.

  Donna Xuan Linh Lee studies ESL in LaGuardia Community College's Chinatown Program in New York City.

B. Tell the class if you agree or disagree with Donna. Explain why.
Talk about your personal experience.

Agreeing	Disagreeing
I agree with her.	I disagree with her.
I think she's right.	I can't agree.
I feel the same way.	I'm not sure if I agree.

Expressing Certainty
I know (that) . . .
I'm sure (that) . . .
I'm certain (that) . . .
In my experience . . .

C. Write your feelings about life in North America, both positive and negative. Complete the sentences below. Use some of the words and phrases in the box if you wish.

I'm satisfied with _____.

I'm pleased with _____.

I enjoy _____.

I'm unhappy about _____.

I'm worried about _____.

I'm afraid of _____.

my job
my children's education
my housing
crime in this country
discrimination
my life here
losing my job
learning English
drugs and gangs
money
my salary
my opportunities
my social life

Read your sentences to a partner.

This is what Andreas Carranza wrote.

I'm satisfied with _My job in Tucson_.

I'm pleased with _my new friends_.

I enjoy _learning English_.

I'm unhappy about _North American food_.

I'm worried about _my family far away_.

I'm afraid of _the crime here_.

Andreas Carranza is from Honduras.
He works in Tucson, AZ.

Other Voices
from North America

A. Work with a partner. Choose one of the stories to read. After two minutes, close your books and retell the story to your partner.

B. Read the other story.

C. Circle words you want to remember.

I am one of the Kurdish people who escaped from Iraq in the spring of 1991. We went to a refugee camp in Turkey. We stayed two years and two months in the camp. Then I came to Canada.

Conditions there were so bad you can't imagine. We were living in tents, and in the summer it was very hot and in the winter there was snow. We didn't have anything, just our tents. When we first came through the mountains—I think you saw that on TV—we thought we would have a new life. We never thought it would be so difficult. I can never forget, not in my whole life.

In my family, we were 24 people—me, my eight brothers and their families, my two sisters, and my mother. For three days we didn't eat anything, because we couldn't get any food. It was 15 or 20 days before enough supplies and food arrived. Every day we could see 20 or 25 people dying, especially old people and babies, because babies need food every day and they couldn't get it, and the old men couldn't continue their lives because it was too difficult.

Savgan Said is from Iraq. He studies ESL in Toronto, Ontario, at Holy Name School.

I came here alone, by myself. I was in Yugoslavia for nine months before that. When the Canadian Embassy there called me for an interview, I was really happy, but I thought, "I'm crazy. Where am I going?" I never knew anything about the Canadian people or the place. Growing up in Albania, we didn't know anything about the West.

I got to Yugoslavia by swimming across a river named Buna on January 18, 1991. I was really cold; I never felt anything like it in my life. It was 150 meters wide. I was with my friend and we helped each other. The people in Yugoslavia were very good; they put us in a refugee camp for six months, and then they sent us to a hotel.

Before I arrived in Canada, I was very scared about coming to the West. In Albania we grew up afraid of people in the West. But when I arrived in Newfoundland, it was the first time in my life that I saw people smiling. They were very friendly to me. And I didn't speak English, not a word.

Sadette Cakalli is from Albania. She studies ESL in Toronto, Ontario, at Holy Name School.

9 Bringing the Outside in: All about Our Countries

Teach the class something about your native country.
Bring to class one of the following items:

1. a memento from your country
2. a picture of a place in your country
3. information about a famous person
from your country

Guatemalan accepts Nobel Prize

The Associated Press

OSLO, Norway — Indian rights activist Rigoberta Menchu accepted the Nobel Peace Prize on Thursday, calling it a tribute to exploited people in her native Guatemala and around the world.

"Today we must fight for a better world, without poverty, without racism, with peace," said Menchu, clad in colorful, striped clothes traditionally worn by Guatemalan Indians.

The 33-year-old laureate won the $973,000 prize for her efforts to bring peace and reconciliation to Guatemala. Some 120,000 people, including Menchu's parents and brother, have died in the Central American country's three decades of civil war.

The award coincided with the 500th anniversary of Columbus's arrival in America. For Menchu and others, 1492 marks the beginning of centuries of violent repression. "I consider this prize not as an award to me personally, but rather as one of the greatest conquests in the struggle for peace, for human rights and for the rights of the indigenous people, who, along all the 500 years, have been ... the victims of genocides, repression and discrimi-

RIGOBERTA MENCHU: "I consider this prize not as an award to me personally, but rather as one of the greatest conquests in the struggle for peace, for human rights and for the rights of the indigenous people ..."

AP PHOTO

nation," she said.

"Let there be freedom for Indians ... because while they are alive, a glow of hope will be alive as well," she said.

The choice of Menchu as the 1992 recipient was controversial because she has been accused of having ties to armed rebel groups in Guatemala. She claims that anyone who campaigns for human rights in her country is called a rebel.

Menchu said she dreams of equal-

ity between the peoples of the world.

"This Nobel Prize is a recognition to those who have been, and still are in most parts of the world, the most exploited of the exploited ones, the most discriminated of the discriminated ones," she told the audience in the crowded Oslo City Hall.

Menchu asked Burma's generals to release the 1991 Nobel Peace Prize winner, Aung San Suu Kyi, who has been under house arrest for

Ideas for Action: Teaching about Our Countries

Most Americans don't know much about Laos. They say, "Isn't it somewhere near Vietnam?" Some think most Southeast Asians are on welfare. They have no idea how hard we work to make a living here.

Chanthava Chanthavong is from Laos and lives in Sunderland, MA.

How can you teach people about your culture or your native country? What are some ways to educate them?

With the class or a small group, brainstorm some ideas.

1. _____We can show a book about our country._____

2. _____

3. _____

4. _____

11 Looking Back

Think about your learning. Complete this form. Then tell the class your ideas.

A. The most useful thing I learned in this unit was _____

_____.

B. I would still like to learn _____.

C. I learned the most by working . . .

_____ alone.   _____ with a partner.   _____ with a group.

D. The activity I liked best was   1   2   3   4   5   6   7   8   9   10

because _____.

E. The activity I liked least was   1   2   3   4   5   6   7   8   9   10

because _____.

Word Bank

Choose eight new words or expressions from this unit that you want to remember. Use them in sentences of your own.

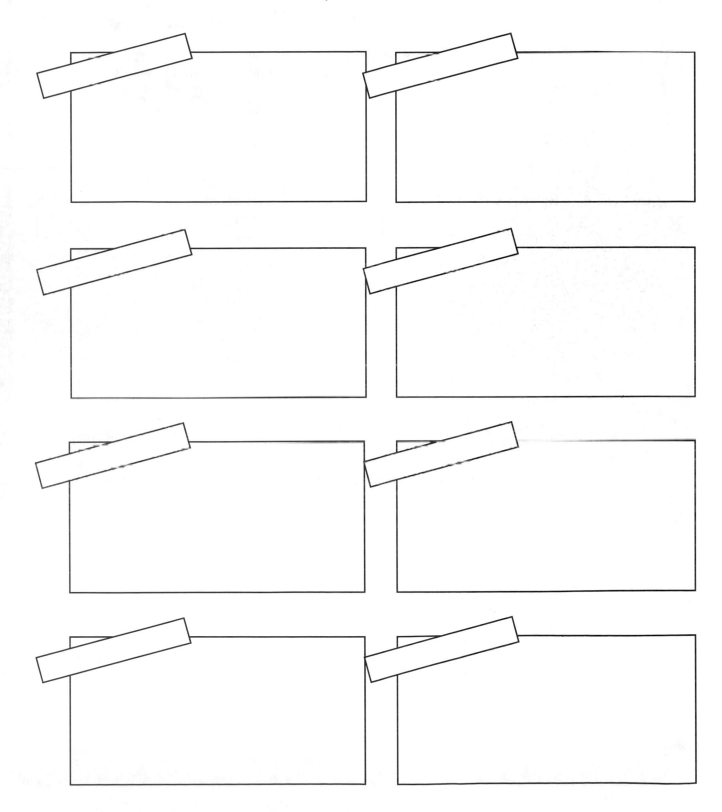

Checklist for Learning

I.   Vocabulary: Check (✔) the words and phrases you know. Add more words and phrases if you wish. For extra practice, write sentences with the words.

Past Verbs

_____ met
_____ pushed
_____ swam
_____ died
_____ traveled
_____ escaped
_____ paid
_____ landed
_____ immigrated

_____ _____
_____ _____

Modes of Transportation

_____ car
_____ truck
_____ fishing boat
_____ ocean liner
_____ rowboat
_____ raft
_____ bus
_____ plane
_____ helicopter

_____ _____
_____ _____

Expressions

_____ be satisfied with
_____ be pleased with
_____ be unhappy about
_____ be worried about
_____ be afraid of

IDIOMS

_____ be blue
_____ make a living

II.   Language: Check (✔) what you can do in English. Add more ideas if you wish.

I can

_____ tell about my trip to North America.
_____ tell my reasons for coming to North America.
_____ agree and disagree with different opinions.
_____ express satisfaction and dissatisfaction.
_____ express worry.
_____ tell about a person, place, or thing from my country.

III.   Listening: Listen to the Review Interview at the end of Unit 6. Ask your teacher for a *Collaborations* worksheet.

INDEX

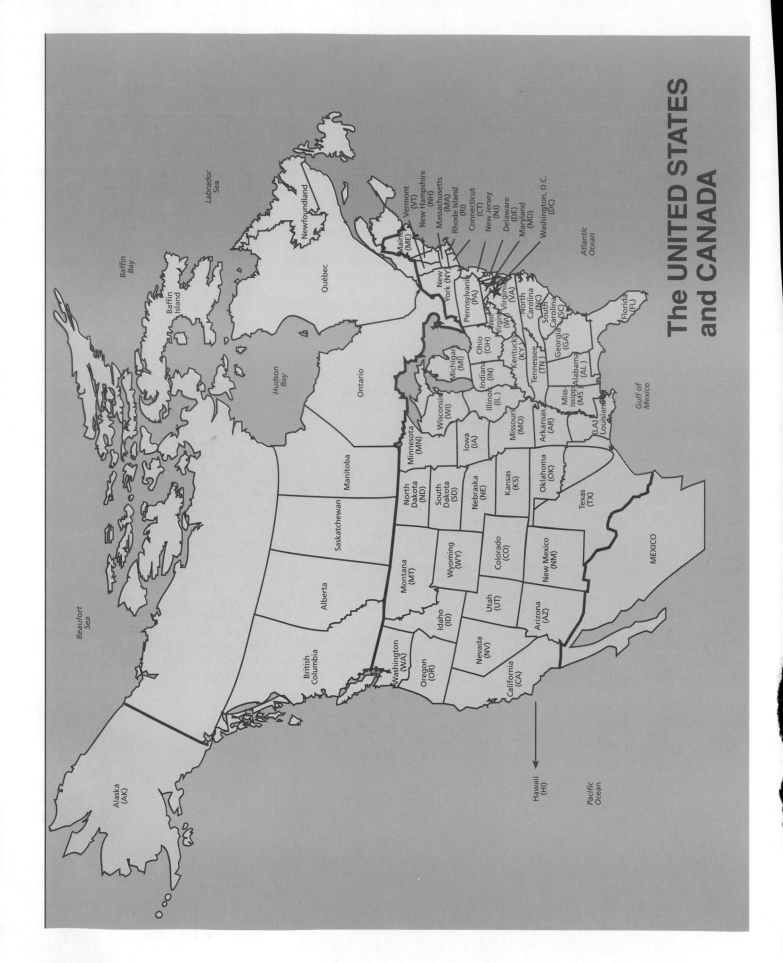

The UNITED STATES and CANADA